ESTHER & MORDECAI'S

House of Redemption

by Marion Reid

CRIMOND
HOUSE

CRIMOND HOUSE PUBLICATIONS

This edition © Copyright 2016 Crimond House Publications
Text © Copyright 2016 Marion Reid

Published in 2016 by
Crimond House Publications
A division of
Ards Evangelical Bookshop
"Crimond House"
48 Frances Street
Newtownards
Co. Down
BT23 7DN
www.ardsbookshop.com

Printed in Glasgow by Bell & Bain Ltd.
Typesetting and cover design by Crimond House Publications.

All rights reserved. No part of this publication may be reproduced, stored in a retrieval system, or transmitted in any form or by any means, electronic, mechanical, photocopying, recording or otherwise, without the prior permission of the copyright owner.

Scripture taken from the Holy Bible,
NEW INTERNATIONAL VERSION®, NIV® Copyright © 1973, 1978, 1984, by Biblica, Inc.® Used by permission. All rights reserved worldwide.

ISBN: 978 1 908618 12 2

Acknowledgements

Writing a book involves many people apart from the author. It would not be possible for me to even begin this project were it not for those who have taught me the scriptures by their own example of Christian living or through the preaching of God's Word. To all of you who have touched my life in such fashion and in so many ways, I say thank-you.

There are of course those who have played a part in this publication without whose help it would not have come to fruition;

My good friend Olive Gardiner who has been my very patient, encouraging and enthusiastic teacher of English grammar. She has spent many hours reading the manuscript and graciously correcting my 'schoolboy' errors. Her invaluable contribution cannot go without mention.
Thank-you Olive.

Ricky McCoubrey of Crimond House Publications, for the time he has taken out of his already busy schedule of commitments to give attention to my writing and, who once again, has given me an opportunity to realize my dream.
Forever grateful.

To Ruth, Vi and Averil, who gave time and attention to the words of this book and responded with their encouraging comments.
Much appreciated.

Other books by Marion Reid
Crimond House Publications:
Ruth & Naomi's House of Bread

Maranatha series:
(available from the author)
But God
A Beautiful Thing
After the Storm

Marion can be contacted by:
Email: maranatha30@talktalk.net
Text or phone: 07443924825

"The book of "Esther", in the Old Testament, does not mention God's name at all! It reads like a thriller! We are introduced to "Baddies," "Goodies," "royalty," "plots," and "treason," but God's hand can be seen through it all. As Mordecai said; Esther had come to royal position, "for such a time as this," and she was willing to lay down her life for her people. I hope you will enjoy this exciting story and recognise the presence of God in every place."
Olive Gardiner

"Like the archaeologist digging in the streets of ancient Babylon, so the Lord has enabled Marion to unearth hidden treasures from the book of Esther that will bless your soul. As you read Esther & Mordecai's House of Redemption you will be challenged to walk closer to the Lord and encouraged that God is always in control. As you make the beautiful prayers the desire of your own heart you will be drawn right into the presence of our "great, wonderful, powerful, redeeming God." There is a lovely cohesiveness to each of the thoughts- testament to the unity of Scripture."
Vi Dawson, Ballymena

"Walk with Marion through the story of Esther and Mordecai. Pick up the treasures of wisdom. Pause a while over the Scriptures quoted. Ponder the prayers before making them your own. Then, walk on with delight in the God Who still transfoms places of despair into houses of redemption."
Ruth Hamilton, Lurgan

"If you are looking to be blessed, challenged and reminded of God's sovereignty in all things... this is it! Totally engrossed in this book, it transported me right into the palace, alongside Esther and Mordecai."
Averil Neilly

Dear Reader,

The Biblical story of Esther introduces us to an orphan child who grew up to become queen in one of the world's largest kingdoms during the reign of King Xerxes in 483 B.C.
Few people ascend a royal throne who are not of royal blood, but Esther's accession came about because of the angry, impulsive and evil desires of both the King and his royal advisors.
This story delivers on every level, as we read of intrigue, conspiracy, manipulation and dishonour. All of which propel Esther and Mordecai into a state of total dependence upon the God of Israel. We witness Mordecai displaying profound grief for his nation and Esther driven to the place of prayer and self-sacrifice.
Although God is not mentioned throughout the Book of Esther in our Bibles, it is impossible to read the story and fail to recognize His fingerprints.
As you read this book may your mind be alert to the work of God in each of the characters, so that this may overflow into your own life with the realisation that He is also at work in you, perfecting those things which He purposed in eternity past.

If the wind suddenly changes and you are turned in a different direction - fear not
God is still in control

If the circumstances look bleak and you feel crushed on every side - fear not
God is still in control

If your heart is breaking and the path before you is dark - fear not
God is still in control

If you are in doubt about anything, cannot work it out or feel confused- fear not
God is still in control

Power and Pleasure

Pride and Prejudice

Prayer and Praise

Preface

There aren't too many pupils in school who would say they, 'absolutely love history!' For many, history is seen as a boring subject. Having to learn and recall dates, places, names of conquerors and of the vanquished, often results in moans and sighs from some, while at the same time, there are those who 'absolutely love history.' I was one of those who sighed! Yet, 'I absolutely love history!'

I love history because it is, '**His** (God's) Story.'

The Bible is a book full of history. It tells us of the creation of the universe, the fall of man, and of God's Redemption story. It is **His** Story from beginning to end. Each book within its covers reveals to us the work of God and His plans and purposes for mankind.

The Book of Esther is one such book in which we are invited into the luxury of a palace and introduced to some of the occupants. As we walk through halls of marble, mother-of-pearl, and other costly stones, surrounded by marble pillars and linen curtains, we will learn about the lifestyle of a king who loved himself and cared little for others. At the stroke of a pen, men and women alike, were either elevated in position, or delivered to death. Power, dominance, greed, conspiracy and intrigue, echo throughout the sumptuous surroundings of the palace in the citadel of Susa. We will cringe as we meet some of the characters and be alarmed at the depths of evil to which they can plunge. We will applaud others who loved God and cared deeply about His plans more than their own lives. Most of all, our hearts will be warmed in the knowledge that our God loves us with an everlasting love and that His faithfulness endures forever.

History, especially the history of the Bible, leaves us in awe of the One who wrote its every letter, word, sentence and paragraph, because, **He** walks through its pages and, **He** speaks through its message.

Unlike other history books, the Bible is alive! When we read and study it, it has instant effect because it is active and up to date. The characters in a sense, are often a reflection of ourselves and our situations. Through them, we can find the strength, comfort, motivation or challenge necessary for day to day living.

So, let's do **His**tory!

Come with me for a walk through

ESTHER & MORDECAI'S

House

of

Redemption

Power and Pleasure

Clap your hands, all you nations:
shout to God with cries of joy.
How awesome is the LORD Most High
the great King over all the earth!
He subdued nations under
us, peoples under our feet.
He chose our inheritance for us,
the pride of Jacob, whom He loved.
Selah
God has ascended amid shouts of joy,
the LORD amid the sounding of trumpets.
Sing praises to God,
sing praises.
For God is the King of all the earth:
sing to him a psalm of praise.
God reigns over the nations;
God is seated on his holy throne.
The nobles of the nations assemble as the
people of the God of Abraham,
for the kings of the earth belong to God;
He is greatly exalted.
    Psalm 47

The King's Banquet/s

Esther 1:2,3
At that time King Xerxes reigned from his royal throne in the citadel of Susa, and in the third year of his reign he gave a banquet for all his nobles and officials. The military leaders of Persia and Media, the princes, and the nobles of the provinces were present.

Here was a man who certainly knew how to throw a party! The military leaders probably came and went throughout the 180 days as and when they could be relieved from duty in their various areas of command. Nevertheless, it seems obvious that the whole idea behind the King's banquet was to display his military prowess and control in the vast area over which he had power. Meeting with his military leaders to discuss plans and possibilities in the sumptuous surroundings of the palace at Susa while showing off his vast wealth, splendour, glory and majesty would add to his already inflated ego. Of course one banquet wasn't enough so another one was given at the end of the 180 days! This time it was for those who lived in the citadel of Susa, from the least to the greatest and it lasted for 7 days. Being king over such a vast kingdom Xerxes was certainly in the mood for displaying his wealth and lavish surroundings to one and all.

The seven-day banquet was held in the enclosed garden of the king's palace. The Bible gives us an account of the beautiful decor in which the guests languished. Linen curtains, marble pillars, gold and silver couches, mosaic pavements of various costly stones. What a wonderful sight this garden would have been; breath-taking in its beauty, rich in its splendour and declaring to all that it belonged to King Xerxes, King of Persia and Media. The guests were served wine in goblets of gold, each one different from the other. Not only that but the wine was abundant and, we read, that this was in keeping with the king's liberality. Xerxes certainly enjoyed indulgence but did not impose this on anyone else, as we are told, he commanded everyone to drink in their own way and the stewards were to serve only what each guest wished or ordered (v.8).

In the Book of Proverbs we read of the advice given to King Lemuel from his mother;

> *"It is not for kings, O Lemuel -*
> *not for kings to drink wine,*
> *not for rulers to crave beer,*
> *lest they drink and forget what the law decrees,*
> *and deprive all the oppressed of their rights...."*
> *Proverbs 31:4*

Sound advice indeed for one who would be a role model as well as ruler. King Xerxes would have benefited greatly from these same words as his 'liberality' with alcohol would very soon lead to him being embarrassed before his drunken guests and subsequently losing his wife! Pride comes before a fall and King Xerxes was certainly going to come down with a bump!

*King of Kings and Lord of Lords
we come before you today
with thankful hearts.
Every good and perfect gift
comes from You.
You own the cattle on a thousand hills
and all we have belongs to you.
May we, with grateful hearts
and praising lips
always acknowledge
Your hand of blessing.*

The heart of the wise is in the house of mourning,
but the heart of fools is in the house of pleasure.
It is better to heed a wise man's rebuke
than to listen to the song of fools.
Like the crackling of thorns under the pot,
so is the laughter of fools.
      Ecclesiastes 7:4-6

The King's Command

Esther 1:10,11
On the seventh day, when King Xerxes was in high spirits from wine, he commanded the seven eunuchs who served him....to bring before him, Queen Vashti, wearing her royal crown...

Seven days of feasting, bragging and drinking has the most powerful ruler in Persia and Media in a state of intoxication. The one item in his display cabinet, which he has yet to show his guests, is the most beautiful woman in the realm, his wife, Queen Vashti. He decides it is time to present her to them.

She, too, was having a banquet for the women. No doubt being queen brought its benefits, but it also brought with it a deep sense of loneliness and possibly boredom. Queen Vashti was not the only female in the royal court who made the king's days pleasurable. She may have been queen but she was also just 'another.' As she hosted the banquet she was interrupted by the king's attendants who delivered the command for her to come to the banquet of the king. For King Xerxes to suggest such a thing was an insult to his queen and so, to their dismay she refused!

Queen Vashti was a very beautiful woman but one who knew only too well how a room full of drunken men could behave. She had no intention of being paraded like a prized animal, possibly in a state of undress, in order to satisfy the impulsive desires of her intoxicated husband. Regardless of hosting 180 days of visiting military leaders, nobles and officials and 7 days seven of partying with the locals of Susa, the queen's refusal has the palace of King Xerxes in total disarray and the whole situation is turned on its head. Xerxes needed to redeem himself and very quickly at that.

The king's reaction was one of burning anger. How embarrassed he must have been in front of all his guests and in his own palace at that! This is not something he was expecting to happen and he had no idea how to handle it. In his inebriated state and rage the only thing he was concerned about now was his reputation. He needed to consult those who were acquainted with matters of law and justice, so he called for seven of his close associates, men who were experts in such things.

Sadly, the man who was ruler of such a large kingdom and held control over so many people of all races and cultures, was now reduced to one who had no control over himself because of his excess indulgence in alcohol. With his mind incapable of conduct befitting one of such status, the king behaved in a very foolish manner and is now seen as a man who has underestimated his wife Vashti and her principles.

King of Kings and Lord of Lords, may we know what it is to be self-controlled and live our lives in such a way as to glorify You. Angry outbursts, pride and revenge are the very essence of self-destruction and not the way to holiness or wholeness. Help us to develop the fruit You desire to see on display as Your representatives - love, joy, peace, patience, kindness, goodness, faithfulness, gentleness and self-control. Against such things there is no law. (Galatians 5:22,23)

*Do not get drunk on wine,
which leads to debauchery.
Instead, be filled with the Spirit
Ephesians 5:18*

You are not a God who takes pleasure in evil;
with you the wicked cannot dwell.
The arrogant cannot stand in your
presence;
you hate all who do wrong.
You destroy those who tell lies;
bloodthirsty and deceitful men the LORD
abhors.
Not a word from their mouth can be
trusted;
their heart is filled with destruction.
Their throat is an open grave;
with their tongue they speak deceit.
Declare them guilty, O God!
Let their intrigues be their downfall.
Banish them for their many sins,
for they have rebelled against you.
    Psalm 5:4-6,9,10

The King's Question

Esther 1:15
"According to law, what must be done to Queen Vashti....?"

King Xerxes called for those who could advise him regarding the refusal of Queen Vashti to come to his banquet as he had commanded. These were seven men who had special access to him and who would also advise the king on matters relating to the State. The Bible refers to them as 'wise men who understood the times.' This seems to suggest they were astrologers who consulted the stars and used other methods of divination. The book of Daniel gives us several verses which indicate that men such as these were used by kings of the east to give instruction in all things military, personal and governmental. (Daniel 1:20;2:2,10,17; 4:7; 5:7, 11,17) The law of the Persians and Medes was such that even the king was subject to it, therefore, he couldn't carry out a punishment on Vashti without consulting the law.

When they came in to the king's presence Xerxes posed a question, *"According to law, what must be done to Queen Vashti, she has not obeyed the command of King Xerxes that the eunuchs have taken to her?"* One of the seven, Memucan, spoke up and gave a speech which was impulsive, exaggerated and very persuasive. He made out that Vasthi's conduct not only affected the king but would have a knock on effect on every husband in the empire! He suggested that those who were in attendance at the banquet would carry the story far and wide and, as a result, all the women would rebel against their husbands and there would be no end of disrespect and discord. These words came from the heart of a man whose ego was quite inflated. As he was only one of a group of seven it seems they were all taking advantage of the king's dependence upon them. Self-seeking and proud of their position in the Royal Court they were now using the art of manipulation to keep them in that position. The king, in their hands, was only a puppet on a string and they knew it. Their opportunity to enhance their status came with the king's question and they were going to make full use of it.

One woman refused the invitation from her husband to come to a party and they turned it into a national crisis! In making this suggestion to the king, they laid the foundation for what was to come and so they gave their collective answer. *"Therefore, if it please the king, let him issue a royal decree and let it be written in the laws of Persia and Media, which cannot be repealed, that Vashti is never again to enter the presence of King Xerxes. Also let the king give her royal position to someone else who is better than she. Then when the king's edict is proclaimed throughout all his vast realm, all the women will respect their husbands, from the least to the greatest."*

According to these 'wise men,' Vashti was disrespectful and disobedient towards the king and her 'bad' influence would have far reaching consequences! They gave no consideration to her own self-respect and self-control which are matchless qualities in any woman. What a role model she really was. If anyone was disrespectful it was Xerxes but these men didn't wish to see it that way. It wasn't just the king's reputation at stake here, it was theirs also.

In this same way, husbands ought to love their wives as their own bodies. He who loves his wife loves himself.
Ephesians 5:28

*King of Kings we come to-day to One who looks upon
each one of us as being precious in Your sight.
Whose thoughts towards us are
good, pure and honourable.
Whose love for us is vast,
unmeasurable and unfathomable.
You desire us to be conformed to the likeness of Your
own Beloved Son Jesus whose life displayed the
qualities we too are exhorted to exemplify.
Things which are true, noble, right,
pure, lovely, admirable,
excellent or praiseworthy. (Philippians 4:8)*

Blessed is the man who does not walk in the counsel of the wicked.
>Psalm 1:1a

The lips of a king speak as an oracle, and his mouth should not betray justice.
A king's wrath is a messenger of death, but a wise man will appease it.
>Proverbs 16:10,14

The King's Edict

Esther 1:22
He sent dispatches to all parts of his kingdom, to each province in its own script and to each people in its own language, proclaiming in each people's tongue that every man should be ruler over his own household.

What a sad ending to the king's days of partying! Still in a state of anger and embarrassment Xerxes agreed to the advice given by Memucan and without even taking time to ponder the suggestion, in his impulsiveness, he signed on the dotted line. This was a king who didn't really care what he was signing as he foolishly trusted the word of his advisors and those around, who could skilfully deliver a speech to serve their own interests. This will not be the only time we shall see the king adding his signature to a document because of the craftiness of others. All he was concerned about was getting the revenge which his anger demanded regarding the queen's refusal to come to the banquet. With the stroke of the pen, Queen Vashti has now been removed from her royal position and will live out her days in obscurity and never again be allowed to come into the presence of the king. She has paid a high price for disobeying the king's command but losing her crown is not as bad as losing her head! Her husband Xerxes, in a sense, lost his head by agreeing to the foolish and callous suggestion of his wise men. He had allowed his moods to dictate his actions in order that he could be seen to be in complete control. What a foolish man he was! Yet it is often the case when we allow our own thoughts, feelings and emotions to take over that our true selves rise to the surface and reveal the intentions of the heart. Xerxes was a proud, impulsive, foolish and arrogant man who cared little for the feelings of others. Under the influence of alcohol and in an angry state, common sense was ruled out and the king suddenly found himself without a queen.

In sending out the edict, King Xerxes was giving men all over his kingdom, rights and privileges, which potentially amounted to domestic abuse and sexual violence towards women. On the other hand; leaving himself without a queen opened up the way for God to show how *His* Sovereign rule and providential acts in history will not be thwarted.

How quickly the fun and the joviality of a party can be replaced by absolute madness. Sadly, this is what alcohol can do. There are men and women who have lost their home, bank account, job, health, spouse, children, and possibly several other significant relationships to the draw of indulging in the world of alcohol. All too often we see T.V adverts showing young, smiling, happy faces enjoying their drinks amongst the bright lights of sumptuous surroundings but what the adverts don't show are the *results* of indulgence and addiction.

A wise man's heart guides his mouth, and his lips promote instruction.
Proverbs 16:23

King of Kings and LORD *of* LORDS,
*there are times in our lives
when we are asked to give our advice.
May we realise that advice
always effects a number of people,
not just the one who asks for it.
With humility and grace
help us to seek Your counsel
before we enter into the realm of counsel ourselves.
Help us also not to be manipulated,
or to manipulate others
into making decisions too quickly
and then suffer the consequences of our error.
Give us the wisdom we need to choose
wisely,
intelligently
and with discretion
and integrity.*

The king's heart is in the hand of the LORD; He directs it like a watercourse wherever he pleases.
        Proverbs 21:1

No Queen

Esther 2:1
Later when the anger of King Xerxes had subsided, he remembered Vashti and what she had done and what he had decreed about her.

It has been approximately three years since Queen Vashti was deposed, during which time the king had embarked on a military campaign against Greece. This endeavour turned out to be a humiliating defeat. Now, as he sits licking his wounds, his thoughts turn once again to Vashti. There may have been many occasions when he reflected upon his angry, drunken moment which led to her removal. The word 'remembered' in this context, suggests, that the king was thinking *affectionately* of her. We have already learned that Vashti was a very 'beautiful' woman and 'lovely' to look upon. Xerxes is missing her! He misses her beauty and her presence in his life. Regardless of his having a harem full of concubines, Vashti had been his queen and the one who completed the King and Queen duo. Alas, because of his irrevocable decree, Vashti could not be reinstated, as even the King became a slave to his own rules. Sharing the matter with his personal attendants probably caused a surge of fear and trepidation amongst them. They were concerned that the king, now regretting his actions, would seek revenge on them! Once again they had to think very quickly!

Turning to the King they said, *"Let a search be made for beautiful young virgins for the King"* (2:2)

A new queen would distract Xerxes from any thought of Vashti and their advice appealed to him. What's new! When the suggestion was made to get rid of Vashti, the King, without giving any forethought as to the effect or outcome this would have upon his subjects, signed the decree which would ultimately leave all the women of the kingdom subject to the abuse of their male counterparts. Now, from these same advisors, comes the suggestion of how Vashti could be replaced. It pleased the king but would bring with it, a frightening and sad experience for every parent and young girl throughout the realm. Once again the puppet king responds to those who serve their own interests.

In childhood, little girls often play 'princesses' and 'queens.' The grandeur and sophistication along with the thought of living in a palace, not to mention a handsome prince, is very alluring. For some, the dream may become a reality one day, who knows! It wouldn't have entered their thoughts that royal living could include men like King Xerxes and his advisors! Selfish, arrogant and ruthless men, such as these, are not played out in childish dreams and imaginations. Now though, having listened, liked and agreed with the advice given, King Xerxes is about to round up young girls and women, who will become his pleasure toys under the guise of selecting a new queen. For some, who perhaps played out this childhood dream it will soon become a nightmare!

Therefore, as we have opportunity, let us do good to all people, especially to those who belong to the family of believers.
Galatians 6:10

King of Kings and LORD *of* LORDS,
*Your word encourages us to lay aside self
in order that we please You
in all our ways.
To put away selfish desires and habits
and look to You so that
we can have all our needs fulfilled.
Give us the grace we need today to live out
love, compassion and mercy
towards all with whom we come into contact.
May they see Jesus in us
as we open our hearts
and hands
to give, from selfless motives,
and not for reason of selfish pride or gain.
Give us a fresh desire in all we do
o bless others and glorify Your Name.*

I know the LORD secures justice for the poor and upholds the cause of the needy.
Psalm 140:12

The Search for a New Queen

Esther 2:2,3
Let a search be made for beautiful young virgins for the King. Let the King appoint commissioners in every province of his realm to bring all these beautiful girls into the harem at the citadel of Susa.

King Xerxes sent out another edict and once again the kingdom was infiltrated with palace officials who on this occasion, had the authority to bring back to Susa beautiful young virgins. There would have been parents who were delighted that they had a suitable candidate in their 'beautiful' young daughter and would have been pleased to see her going off with the king's officials. Yet, I can imagine the panic and fear in the homes of some with daughters of marriageable age. Parents who would be only too aware that once their beloved daughter or daughters were taken away, they would never see them again! Perhaps some lied when their doors were knocked by the king's men. Others may have even hidden their daughters. Some of the young girls themselves may have hidden away in fear of what lay ahead. There may have been those who were already engaged to be married and for their young men, their bride would be stolen away! This whole exercise was not a beauty competition as we have come to know beauty competitions. This was a national 'round up' of girls throughout the vast kingdom of Xerxes in search of a new queen. Young women who would be used by the king to satisfy his sensual desires and none of whom would leave the confines of the harem again or ever have an opportunity of one day becoming a bride. For those who were brought back to Susa, a year would pass before they went in to the king. It is good to remind ourselves of the reason they were brought to the citadel at Susa - to replace Vashti as queen - yet there is no mention of them being trained in 'queenly' things. Instead, they would spend twelve months being pampered with various oils, perfumes and cosmetics, preparing themselves physically for the ultimate position in the kingdom which would bring the chosen one privileges beyond her dreams. Regardless of the fact that they were already 'beautiful' young women, it seemed necessary to add to that beauty! Each one of them would have hoped she would be the 'one' and during the twelve months it probably did turn out to be a beauty contest amongst themselves and, like all young woman in every generation, they would have enjoyed the pampering, along with trying on the stunning clothes which were also provided. When the time came, the Bible tells us that, *'In the evening she would go there, and in the morning return to another part of the harem...She would not return to the king unless he was pleased with her and summoned her by name.'* (2:14)

What a sad verse this is! After their 'interview' with the king, these girls would now spend the rest of their lives in obscurity. Some would live in the concubine's quarters with the slim chance of being called to the king again. Those who didn't ever get the invitation into the king's chambers, were possibly locked away in an area set aside for the women. It would be good to think though, that many were allowed to go home again. On leaving the king's presence, each girl would have known she was not chosen to be queen. The disappointment, sense of abandonment and rejection amongst them must have been tangible. Any dreams and aspirations they had prior to this event were now most definitely put away for good... just as they were. What a price to pay for being beautiful!

Using other people for our own advantage or pleasure is in disobedience to what the Word of God has to say regarding the treatment of our fellow man. Xerxes and his advisors will one day be held accountable before God for their actions towards these young women. I sometimes wonder how quickly the advisors will come up with a response when *God asks* them to give an account!

For we must all stand before the judgement seat of Christ, that each one may receive what is due to him for the things done in the body, whether good or bad.
1 Corinthians 5:10

King of Kings we come before You today in the knowledge that all Your thoughts towards us are good, pure and precious. There are many who use and abuse others for their own sadistic purposes and it is our prayer that You would now come and minister Your grace and healing in any who may be living with past hurts in this area. You know who they are and we pray for Your touch upon them right now. Give them a real sense of Your presence, power and love. May their hearts be warmed in the healing power of the Holy Spirit's ministry as they cry out to You for peace, wholeness and contentment.

Surely, as I have planned, so it will be, and as I have purposed, so it will stand. For the LORD Almighty has purposed, and who can thwart him? His hand is stretched out, and who can turn it back?
      Isaiah 14:24,27

Mordecai the Jew

> **Esther 2:5**
> *Now there was in the citadel of Susa a Jew of the tribe of Benjamin, named Mordecai...*

We are now introduced to Mordecai and his cousin Esther. Their emergence from obscurity would have such an impact upon the unfolding events taking place in the kingdom of Persia in 5th-century B.C. that we, in the 21st-century A.D., can only stand in awe at the foreknowledge and foresight of our Eternal God.

Their ancestors came from the tribe of Benjamin who were deported to Babylon about one hundred years earlier when King Nebuchadnezzar took Jerusalem captive in 597 B.C. (2 Kings 24.) Many years later the Jews were allowed to return to their own land under the decree of King Cyrus, which some of them did. Others followed at a much later stage but there were those who stayed in the land of their captivity (for some, the land of their birth) and it seems Mordecai and his family were amongst that number. Under Persian rule many of the remaining Jews prospered and even rose to high ranking positions in government and business. Mordecai is recorded in Scripture as one who 'sat at the king's gate' which was indeed a prominent position. He adopted Esther when she was orphaned and brought her up as his own daughter. She was his uncle's child but we are not told if she was an only child. He was willing to add her to his household and take responsibility for her upbringing. This, in itself shows us that Mordecai was a man of compassion with a deep sense of responsibility towards his family. It seems obvious from the Biblical narrative, that he taught Esther about her Hebrew history and ancestry, which would have, undoubtedly, included the laws and appointed feasts as given by God. However, it is difficult to comprehend how Mordecai allowed Esther to become a member of the harem of a pagan king!

Was he one of the 'ambitious' parents?
Was he a 'nominal' Jew who compromised his faith in the society in which he lived?
Did he not have a choice?

We are not given this information from Scripture and have no right to speculate on it. What we do know is, that even though God is not mentioned in the Book of Esther, evidence of His sovereignty, providence and overruling power runs throughout the story. We witness His Presence in the lives of the characters and circumstances which occur. Regardless of whether those circumstances were meant for good or evil, His ultimate plans and purposes would not be thwarted by either the thoughts and intentions of evil men and women, or, by unfaithfulness and compromise amongst His own people.

As we read this account of life in Susa, Persia, all those years ago, may we remind ourselves that God is the same yesterday, to-day and forever. The God of Mordecai and Esther is the same God of you and me today! What an encouragement this is to us in our present world of wars, racism, power struggles and persecution.

God's sovereignty, providence and overruling power is fully operational and His plans and purposes will be fulfilled in spite of anything or anyone!

Therefore, we have no cause to fear but are asked to trust Him and to *'Look up!'* (Luke 21:28.)

Heavenly Father, help us to remember always Who is in complete control of everything which happens in this world so that we may continue to serve You with steadfast faith, obedience, courage and with the same attitude as that of the Apostle Paul who said,

I press on towards the goal to win the prize for which God has called me heavenwards in Christ Jesus.
Philippians 3:14

Let the beauty of Jesus be seen in me,
All His wondrous compassion and purity;
Oh, Thou Spirit divine, all my nature refine,
Till the beauty of Jesus be seen in me.
      Albert Orsborn

Esther the Orphan

Esther 2:8
...Esther also was taken to the king's palace and entrusted to Hegai...

On the day Esther entered the palace, Mordecai effectively relinquished his responsibility towards his cousin. Regardless of this he was still very much concerned about her welfare. Esther, for her part, continued in her obedience to Mordecai by not revealing her nationality and family background. Once again, we are left questioning Mordecai's motives.

Esther was her Persian name which means, 'Star'. This was indeed a name which she will certainly live up to as she eventually becomes the 'Star' of the story which is about to unfold.

Her Hebrew name Hadassah, means 'Myrtle.' The myrtle was a Palestinian evergreen which often reached heights of thirty feet. Its fragrant leaves and scented white flowers were used as perfumes. How apt it is then for us to read the account of Esther (Hadassah) who, when taken to the palace and put under the charge of Hegai;

'pleased him and won <u>his</u> favour' (v.9.)
'won the favour of <u>everyone</u> who saw her' (v.15.)
'won the favour and approval' of the <u>king</u> (v.17.)

Esther was 'fragrant' amongst all with whom she came into contact. She obviously lived up to the meaning of her Hebrew name also.
What a testimony!

Adding to this 'fragrance' she was also, *'lovely in form and features'* (v.7.)

Esther brings a refreshing contrast to what has, so far, been a tale of pride, drunkenness, anger, selfishness and oppression. Even though the criteria depended upon the *outward* beauty of the girls taken to Susa, Esther seems to have had an *inward* quality which enhanced her outward loveliness and which captured Hegai's attention. It is not difficult therefore, for us to imagine the thoughts of Hegai who would have known exactly what the king would be looking for. Esther's beauty, elegance and decorum were unsurpassed and he would now set about preparing her to appear before the king in twelve month's time. He began by assigning to her seven maids selected from the king's palace and moved Esther and her maids, into the best place in the harem!

Heavenly Father, what a privilege it is to be invited to call You Father.
When we were orphans and outside of Your family You brought us in.
Jesus who is our Saviour, Redeemer and Friend is also our 'Brother.'
No longer do we lack anything in any area of our lives as You have promised to supply all of our needs.
Your unfailing love surrounds us as You protect, provide and preserve us.
Thank you for the shelter of Your love which covers us, because we stand in the Righteousness of Christ.

***He who dwells in the shelter of the Most High will rest in the shadow of the Almighty.
Psalm 91:1***

Your beauty should not come from outward adornment, such as braided hair and the wearing of gold jewellery and fine clothes. Instead, it should be that of your inner self, the unfading beauty of a gentle and quiet spirit, which is of great worth in God's sight.
    1 Peter 3:3,4

Shine the Light

Matthew 5:16
Let your light so shine before men, that they may see your good works, and glorify your Father which is in heaven.

The Bible encourages those who follow Jesus to, *"let your light shine."* In fact, the Authorised Version says, *"Let your light so shine..."* In other words, we are to *shine* in such a way that others will sit up and take notice. What a challenge this is! As we move through the darkness of the world, our lives should be reflecting the light of God, lighting up that darkness and helping a lost world to see the Father in Heaven. Like Esther, whose demeanour drew people in favour towards her, we too should be attractive for Christ's sake and the Father's glory.

One day I watched a programme on television called Undercover Boss. It was about the CEO of a company disguising himself and visiting the various outlets, factories and shops which the company owned. The purpose was to see how business was delivered on a day to day basis. He worked amongst the staff without them knowing who he was. He discovered problems and heard many ideas which could improve the company's image or profits. He also met with men and women who had amazing personal stories of suffering and struggle. At the end of the programme the boss revealed his true identity much to the shock and surprise of the employees. These men and women were then congratulated, promoted and rewarded for their efforts or for long service and commitment to the company. Their concerns about their children's education or the on-going health expenses incurred while looking after a family member were now lessened because of the generosity of the boss and the rich reward they received.

On that day as I watched, one of the employees, a very humble man who worked in the company, also ran an outreach from his local church. The community programme he ran dealt with folk who had many social as well as personal issues because of poverty, drugs, homelessness, abuse, hunger etc. His work ethic was beyond reproach and his commitment to the community even more so. The boss was very impressed with him and rewarded him generously on a personal level, as well as for the work he did in the community. The employee was overwhelmed by the generosity and sensitivity of the boss towards him and with tears of gratitude running down his face, he said to his boss, *"The Bible says, 'You shall sit among Kings' and today, that's where I am."*
What affected him even more was the response of his boss to that remark when he said, *"It is ME who is sitting among Kings."*
Wow!
Here was the boss of a very large American company who was so impressed by the 'light' which shone from this Christian man's life that *he* was humbled in his presence!
What a challenge!

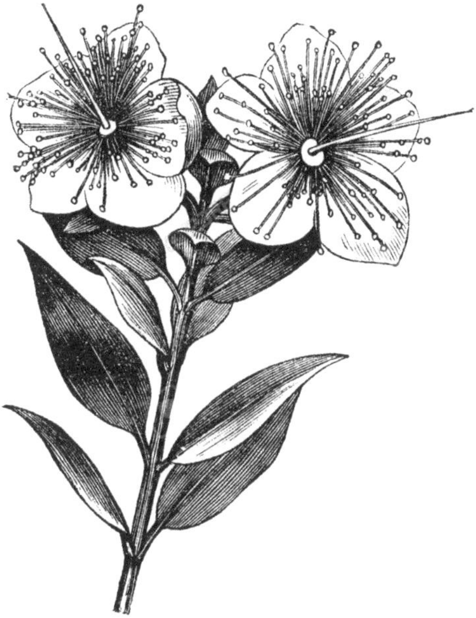

> And God raised us up with Christ and seated us with Him in the heavenly realms in Christ Jesus.
> Ephesians 2:6

The Queen is Chosen

Esther 2:17
Now the king was attracted to Esther more than to any of the other women...

We have already read of Esther's humble up-bringing as an orphaned child in the home of her cousin Mordecai and how she was obedient to his instruction. In the palace and now under the direction and instruction of Hegai, Esther continued to respond with an obedient heart. We are told that when her turn came to go in to the king she asked for nothing other than what Hegai suggested. She was willing to submit herself to his wisdom and knowledge regarding the desire of the king. Not only that, it seems that Esther was content to trust God for the outcome. *'She asked for nothing,'* (v.15,) suggests she had no intention of adding to her beauty.

Here was a young woman whose self-worth came from who she was in God. Esther knew that If God wanted her in the position of queen then it would happen. She did not need to 'mask' herself in make-up, seductive clothing or expensive jewellery. Her decision to go before the king without adding artificial adornment to her already stately demeanour, lovely form and features, had such an impression upon King Xerxes that he chose her as his new queen.

What a change in the life of this young woman! Someone, whose name was probably not of any great interest to anyone in Susa, and now she is the Queen of Persia!

All this the result of the angry outbursts and foolish decisions made by King Xerxes.

Of Hebrew descent, the chosen nation of God, Esther was raised up to one of the most honourable positions in the largest kingdom of the ancient world.

God, the Sovereign Ruler of the universe and the One of whom it says, *"The King's heart is in the hand of the LORD; he directs it like a watercourse wherever he pleases"* (Proverbs 21:1) has now placed His servant Esther into a position of influence. A position in which she will play a major role, as God redirects the course of evil soon to arise against His chosen ones. King Xerxes may have thought he was the one who had chosen his new queen but what he didn't reckon upon was, that, ***Esther was Born to be Queen!***

For he chose us in him before the creation of the world....
Ephesians 1:4

*Heavenly Father, Thank-you for loving me,
forgiving me,
making me Your child
and living in me
through the gift of Your Holy Spirit,
all of which was determined in Eternity past!
May these most precious truths
be the anchor of my soul;
the confidence for daily living
in all and every situation;
faith to believe You will bring about
the right conclusion in times of testing
and the assurance of my worth as an individual.*

Then our sons in their youth will be like well-nurtured plants and our daughters will be like pillars carved to adorn a palace.
	Psalm 144:12

The Queen is Crowned

Esther 2:17
So he set a royal crown on her head and made her queen instead of Vashti.

Vashti has been replaced. A new queen has now been installed in the royal palace and King Xerxes, yet again, throws a party! The king gave a great banquet called *'Esther's banquet'*, in honour of his new Queen. He wanted everyone to celebrate with him, so he invited all his nobles and officials, proclaimed a public holiday throughout the realm and distributed gifts. What an occasion this must have been and especially for Esther the orphaned Hebrew child!

Esther's name was now listed among those whom God uses for the outworking of His purposes;
- Moses was a prince in Egypt.
- Joseph became second in command to Pharaoh.
- Daniel was promoted to third highest ruler in the kingdom of Babylon.
- Nehemiah served as cup-bearer to the king.

There were many others who could be added to this list who were in the right place at the right time due to the providence and sovereignty of Almighty God. Now Esther takes up her position under the eye of this all-seeing, all-knowing God and, like the others, is unaware of the mighty role she is about to play. That her name will be remembered in a book of its own in Scripture and revered by the Hebrew people down through the centuries because of events which are about to unfold, is something Esther is oblivious to as she is being crowned Queen of Persia.

While King Xerxes celebrates what he thinks has been his choice of queen (but has actually been *God's choice,*) let us remember that behind all the pomp, ceremony and extravagance, there is a greater celebration being planned. Hadassah (myrtle) has now been firmly planted in the palace of King Xerxes where she will bloom in the place of God's choosing and be used greatly for the salvation of His chosen people. Both she and Mordecai have access to the royal court and their future actions will change (spiritually speaking) the palace of King Xerxes into a **House of Redemption.**

There are those of us who feel we have insignificant roles in life. I have even heard women respond to the question, *"And what do you do?"* by saying, *"I'm just a stay at home mum."* It's as if their significance depended on not being at home with their children but by having a career! Our significance does not depend upon *what we do* but upon *who we are*! When we bloom where we are planted, we can be used of God to have significant influence on the lives of others whether it is in the home, school or workplace. In God's plan for our lives we are never an, *"I'm just a..."* rather, you and I are of great importance to the ongoing work of God for the salvation of men and women.

And you have been given fulness in Christ,
Who is head over every power and authority.
Colossians 2:10

*Heavenly Father, forgive us when **we look** at
ourselves and only see
inadequacy,
insignificance,
imperfection
or irrelevance.
How good it is to know
that when **You look** at us,
You see preciousness,
potential,
possibility,
promise
and purpose.
We are individuals for whom Christ died,
in order that we may have a future
and a hope.
Because of the great Salvation found in Him
we have become Your children
and therefore are of **great significance**
as we are now also,
members of the Royal Household
of the King of Kings.
Thank You for making us complete in Christ.*

Be sure of this: the wicked will not go unpunished, but those who are righteous will go free.
      Proverbs 11:21

The Plot to Kill the King

Esther 2:21
...two of the King's officers...became angry and conspired to assassinate King Xerxes.

One day as Mordecai was sitting at the king's gate he overheard a conversation between two of the king's officers. The two men, Bigthana and Teresh, were angry and conspired to kill the king. Why these two were angry is not revealed. Maybe they felt the king should have looked for his new queen amongst the nobles and not the 'common' people. Although, not always the case, it was traditional for Persian kings to choose their wives from the seven noble families in the land. Perhaps these men were jealous of Esther becoming queen. Having such an ordinary woman on the throne may have upset their traditional values. Whatever the reason for their state of anger, it had moved beyond an emotional feeling and was now firmly grounded in a murderous plot.

Mordecai told Queen Esther about the plot and she, in turn, reported it to the king giving the credit to Mordecai. On investigation it was discovered that the two men had indeed plotted the king's demise and they were both put to death. The whole story was recorded, along with Mordecai's name in the record books of the king and, in the presence of the king.

It should not escape our notice that anger seems to play a major role in this story. We are reminded in the book of Ephesians, *"In your anger do not sin,"* (Ps.4:4.) *"Do not let the sun go down while you are still angry and do not give the devil a foothold."* (Eph.4:26,27)

The Lord Jesus, while speaking on the mountain one day also mentioned that *"anger will be subject to judgement"*. (Matt.5:22)

Both of these warnings are given because of the terrible consequences which may occur if anger is not brought under control and we have already witnessed the king's responses in his uncontrolled anger!

The first account we have, regarding anger is given to us in the book of Genesis. There we read that Cain was very angry with his brother Abel because his offering was not accepted by God and Abel's was.

When God spoke to Cain about this, His words were plain and simple,

"Why are you angry? Why is your face downcast? If you do what is right, will you not be accepted? But if you do not do what is right, sin is crouching at your door: it desires to have you, but you must master it." (Genesis 4:6,7)

Unfortunately, Cain did not master his anger and as it festered in his heart and mind the result was the murder of his brother.

Angry outbursts leave no room for sensible outcomes as judgement is impaired by the rage within. Wrong decisions are made and often other people are hurt and wounded. On reflection, most people look back and see the error of their ways. Sadly though, the damage has already been done and because anger is usually expressed in words and action, the effect can last for a lifetime for the one at whom the anger has been targeted. Words are spoken which cause deep wounds and broken hearts; relationships are severed and forgiveness becomes difficult for both parties. This was the case in the account of Cain, murder was the result and here in the story of Esther murderous thoughts became the result of angry feelings.

Self-control is the message of the Scriptures and when we lose self-control then we are opening our lives to the effects and consequences of sin. Not only will the result end in brokenness on a human level but our relationship with God will also be broken. Allowing God to have His way in our lives as He moulds and shapes us by His Grace, will give us the confidence and security necessary in order for us to live under His control. This way we will see things from His perspective and not our own. Our reactions will then be God-centred and not self-centred and the reward will be life and not death as was the case with Bigthana and Teresh.

Gracious Father, as You seek to make us more and more into the likeness of Your Beloved Son Jesus, give us the grace necessary to bring under subjection those things which lead to anger in the first place. May we subdue any jealousies, pride, covetousness or anything else which comes into our thoughts and which may lead us into temptation and sin. As we spend time in Your word, show us those thoughts and feelings which need to be taken captive and eradicated. Help us to be open to Your teaching, rebuking, correcting and training in righteousness so that we may be thoroughly equipped for every good work.

**The fruit of the Spirit is self-control.
Galatians 5:23**

The LORD has dealt with me according to my righteousness; according to the cleanness of my hands He has rewarded me.
>   Psalm 18:20

The Plot Recorded

Esther 2:23
All this was recorded in the book of the annals in the presence of the king.

There is no record of Mordecai receiving any reward at this stage for his part in saving the king's life. That would come later. The relationship between Queen Esther and Mordecai is unknown to those within the palace but it will be this particular event which will become pivotal in the whole story when God uses Mordecai's intervention in the plot to gain favour in the eyes of the king.

Mordecai showed his loyalty towards the king in what he did. As an employee of the King of Persia he was faithful to both God and the king while in the workplace.

When Mordecai's ancestors were carried into captivity, the prophet Jeremiah gave them this word from the LORD, *"Also, seek the peace and the prosperity of the city to which I have carried you into exile. Pray to the LORD for it, because if it prospers, you too will prosper."* (Jeremiah 29:7.) Surely this is what Mordecai was doing as he served the king faithfully. Sometimes we fail to recognize that we are to *"Give to Caesar what is Caesar's and to God what is God's"* (Matt.22:21)

Even though several years would pass before any reward would come his way, Mordecai did not seek any in the intervening time. It was now recorded in the king's record and that was that. God, in His own time and in His own way will remember Mordecai.

The Bible speaks of books into which our names and deeds are recorded:
- Book of remembrance - Malachi 3:16
- Book of Life - Philippians 4:3

These are the most important books of all and are **God's record** concerning our lives. If we dwelt too long on thoughts regarding what may be recorded there we would despair, *but*, thanks be to God our Heavenly Father who, in Jesus, wiped the record clean the moment we acknowledged His finished work on the cross for sin. All our sin, past, present and future has been covered in the sacrificial blood which was shed by Jesus when He offered Himself in our place. The grace of God now flows freely into our lives as we seek to serve Him on this earth. The work we do is not ours but His and the strength in which we do it is not ours but His. So let us with grateful hearts glorify His Holy Name in **all** that we do and when the books are opened on that day, may we hear His lovely voice saying, *"Well done, good and faithful servant."*

Heavenly Father, let us not be ever seeking
the praise and adulation of man
for the things which we do
even though those things may include
the saving of another's life.
May our deeds be done to please You
and bring glory to Your Name
and not to ours.
With humility of spirit and kindness of heart
help us to release the love
You have shed abroad in our hearts
purely for the benefit of others.

*Be imitators of God, therefore,
as dearly loved children,
and live a life of love,
just as Christ loved us
and gave Himself up
as a fragrant offering
and sacrifice to God.
Ephesians 5:1,2*

Pride and Prejudice

There are six things the LORD hates,
Seven that are detestable to him:
Haughty eyes,
A lying tongue,
Hands that shed innocent blood,
A heart that devises wicked schemes,
Feet that are quick to rush into evil,
A false witness who pours out lies
And a man who stirs up dissension among brothers.
        Proverbs 6:16-19

Haman's Promotion

Esther 3:1
After these events, King Xerxes honoured Haman...

Anger, deceit, cunning, selfishness and murderous plots have dominated the story so far and it doesn't get any better! We will now encounter one of the most evil of all the characters in the Book of Esther. His name is Haman and he is a man who personifies all those, who, throughout history have raised themselves up against the Hebrew children of God, with the express intent of annihilating the whole race.

Haman was a descendant of King Agag of the Amalekites who were Israel's enemies. We are introduced to them, in the book of Exodus, when they attacked the journeying Israelites on their way to the promised land and sought to prevent them entering Cannan (Exodus 17:18-25.) God had told Moses that He had declared war upon the Amalaekites and that they would be completely blotted out, (Deut. 25:17-19.) Later on, in the history of Israel, King Saul was ordered to destroy them, but he did not obey God's command and he therefore lost his kingship because of his disobedience (1 Samuel 15.) Now, in the story of Esther, we meet up with one of their descendants.

Proverbs 6:16-19 speaks of six things the LORD hates and each one of those things describes Haman perfectly. Everything about him is hateful. Yet, in all of this, King Xerxes promoted him to a position of honour above all other officials in his kingdom. No doubt Haman, who was a wicked, cunning man, probably sweet talked himself into the position. He would have known that the king was easily flattered and persuaded, in any and every direction, if he thought it would bring him more adulation. Now having succeeded in gaining the king's favour, Haman embarked upon a mission of self-promotion and self-assertion. Is it any wonder the Lord recorded in Scripture the following words; *"Do not fret because of evil men or be envious of those who do wrong; for like the grass they will soon wither, like green plants they will soon die away."* Psalm 37:1,2

These are words of encouragement for the child of God, especially when faced with the onslaught of persecution from those who oppose the living God and His purposes for mankind. Esther and Mordecai will soon have to dig deep and remind themselves of these scriptures. Their faith and trust in the God of the Hebrews, will be tested totally and absolutely once the wicked Haman begins to assert himself.

*Heavenly Father, when we consider Your Beloved Son Jesus, whom You raised from the dead and seated at Your right hand, our eyes behold the humble, servant of God, whose obedience in all things, even death on a cross, qualified Him for such an exalted position. May we follow His example of humility and obedience, rather than seeking self-glory. Help us to look towards the cross as we walk our earthly pilgrimage and so keep focused on the fact that we are who we are, because of Who **He** is.*

For in Him
we live
and move
and have our being
Acts 17:28

> When the righteous triumph, there is great elation; but when the wicked rise to power, men go into hiding.
> Proverbs 28:12

Haman's Pride

Esther 3:2
But Mordecai would not kneel down or pay him honour.

Having been promoted to a position, which provided him with great power and authority, Haman delighted in the fact that the king had also commanded everyone to kneel down and honour him as he passed by or appeared in public. It seems reasonable enough to assume that Haman, in his deceitful scheming manner, had written such preferential treatment into his job description! Had the king not given thought to the fact that when he and Haman appeared together in public, Haman would be receiving the same honour as the king himself? Haman knew King Xerxes paid little attention to detail, especially on the written page, so for him to draw up a contract relating to a position which would give him such privileges was easy. King Xerxes, as we have already gathered, signed his name on the dotted line regardless of the outcome his signature commanded.

All the other officials obeyed the king's command and they could not understand why Mordecai did not bow down. So, day after day, they kept on asking Mordecai why he would not kneel down and honour Haman but he refused to give them a reason. Then, there came a day when, perhaps, because of the continuous pressure from their asking, he told them that he was a Jew (v.4.) Mordecai obviously knew that Haman was a descendent of the Amelikites and he probably hated him for being so. For Mordecai, therefore, to kneel and honour such a one was not in his heart or will to do. Unfortunately, the other officials told Haman about Mordecai's behaviour. Perhaps some of them disliked Haman for other reasons and were hoping to get out of doing it themselves! Sadly, though, by reporting Mordecai to Haman, it sparked such anger in the heart of a man who was already consumed by his own self-importance. His conceited, arrogant, proud behaviour would soon rise to a level which would reveal his true character.

The Bible gives several references, in the New Testament, regarding how God's people should honour the king. Two of these can be found in 1Peter 2:17: and Romans 13:1-8. The Old Testament also records many times where the people paid homage to their reigning monarch, even amongst the Jewish race. In the light of this, it is difficult for us to understand Mordecai's motives other than his own personal testimony. Mordecai most likely knelt before the king when required to do so but Haman was not the king. Haman was the enemy. Haman did not deserve Mordecai's honour. That is probably how Mordecai read the situation. He most likely knew what a cunning, scheming man Haman was and he would very soon discover how right he was and also, how much he had underestimated Haman's character!

> *Jesus said,*
> **"I am sending you out like sheep among wolves, therefore be as shrewd as snakes and as innocent as doves."**
> **Matthew 10:16**

*Gracious LORD, as we come before You today,
help us to impress others by the outworking
of the Holy Spirit in our hearts
and not by our own selfish desires and efforts.
Take away the dross and so eliminate those things
which define us in a negative way.
As Your Word washes over our souls,
may we be willing participants in the work You are
doing in our lives.
Carve within us the attributes and characteristics of
our lovely LORD Jesus,
whose desire is for us to display compassion, love and
grace towards others.
Amen.*

In your anger do not sin. Do not let the sun go down while you are still angry.
Ephesians 4:26

Haman's Rage

Esther 3:5
When Haman saw that Mordecai would not kneel down or pay him honour, he was enraged.

It would be foolish, for any one of us, to say we had never been angry at some stage in our lives. All of us are guilty and, on such occasions, we seek to blame our outburst on someone or something else. Because of our insecurities; a perceived threat towards our position, a lack of self-control and the inherent nature of sin, prevent us from throwing our hands in the air and taking responsibility for our anger. Haman's anger was fuelled by his own pride and also the knowledge that Mordecai was a Jew and so, ancestral history raised its ugly head. The hatred he felt towards Mordecai and the power he had to have him put to death for his disobedience, stretched further afield, as Haman began to plot in his heart the eradication of *all* the Jews in the kingdom.

Once again in the palace of King Xerxes anger explodes and as we have already seen, the disobedience of one person, mixed with the anger of the offended one, will effect innocent people all over the kingdom. Haman figured, that if Mordecai got away with not paying honour to him then very soon *all* the Jews throughout the kingdom would follow suit. This would threaten and demean his position and that, was not an option.

Haman was a man, who was just one of several, used of Satan throughout history, who had sought to get rid of God's chosen people and if successful, the nation, through whom the Saviour of the world would come, would be extinct.

Now Satan was trying once more through the wicked schemes of Haman but nothing and no-one, could ever thwart God's plan of salvation in Jesus His Son. As his evil plans unfolded, little did Haman know that God was a step ahead and He had His people in place, Esther was already living in the, **House of Redemption!**

Anger and pride may be ruling in Haman's heart, but *God rules* in the heavens and on the earth.

In the Sermon on the Mount, Jesus said, *"You have heard that it was said to the people long ago, 'Do not murder, and anyone who murders will be subject to judgment.' But I tell you that anyone who is angry with his brother will be subject to judgment."* (Matthew 5:21,22.) From these words, we see that Haman was very quickly moving through the list of things God hates as recorded in Proverbs 6.

*Our Father in heaven, how thrilling it is to know that You are in complete control of all circumstances. Despite the evil intents and purposes of man, You are at work bringing about Your purposes.
How we marvel at Your foreknowledge and foresight. May the impact of this sink deep into our hearts, so that, in the days of weakness and fragile faith, we can be strengthened in spirit and encouraged to rise up with fresh vigour.*

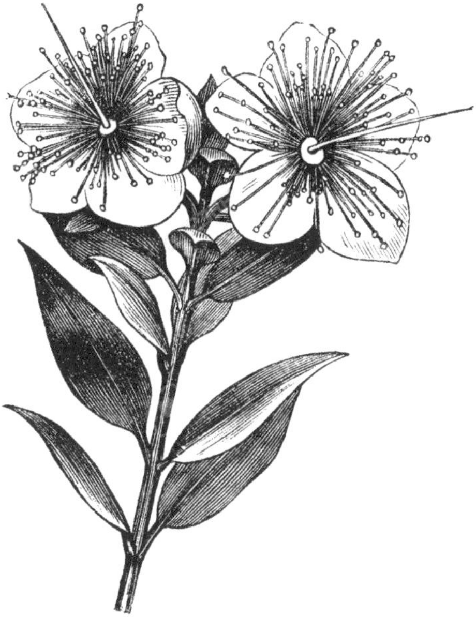

Why do you boast of evil, you mighty man?
Why do you boast all day long?
you who are a disgrace in the eyes of God?
Your tongue plots destruction;
it is like a sharpened razor,
you who practice deceit.
You love evil rather than speaking the truth.
You love every harmful word,
O you deceitful tongue!
Surely God will bring you down to
everlasting ruin:
He will snatch you up and tear you from
your tent;
He will uproot you from the land of the
living.
      Psalm 52:1-4

Haman's Plot

Esther 3:7
And the lot fell on the twelfth month, the month of Adar.

Having figured out how he wanted to deal with Mordecai's public displays of what seemed to be utter abhorrence of him, Haman began to put the wheels of his evil desires into motion. He consulted the astrologers, who cast the pur (that is, the lot,) in his presence, to select a day and a month in which he could carry out his atrocities. Ironically, the Bible records this activity as taking place in the month of Nissan the very month Jews celebrated their deliverance from Egypt. Behind whatever celebrations were to take place in homes across the kingdom, wicked Haman was setting a date for their complete destruction. The lot fell on the twelfth month, the month of Adar.

The decision was made!
The lot had fallen!
The date was chosen!
All Haman needed now, was the king's signature!

The month of Adar was almost a year away. A year in which all the Jews in the kingdom would live in fear of their lives, perhaps move away to somewhere safe or seek ways in which to defend themselves. Haman may have preferred the date to be sooner than this as he would have relished in his swift and sudden slaughter of innocent men, women and children. Being the wicked, evil man he was, a year gave him even more time to excite himself in his power and control, to wallow in his hatred and to dream of the panic and fear he would bring.

Haman would now continue to scheme and plot until his authority, over Mordecai and the Jews of the kingdom, was endorsed by the king but, he is completely unaware of the sovereign power and control that the God of the Hebrews has, in all the affairs of man.

Haman did not know that the Book of Proverbs says; *"The lot is cast into the lap, but its every decision is from the LORD"* (16:33)

Sovereign LORD,
In our distress, You are our Refuge.
In our fear, You are our Peace.
In our weakness, You are our Strength.
In our battles, You are our Shield and Protector.
In our times of doubt, You are our Hope.
In our grief, You are our Comfort.
In our sorrow, You are our Song.

You are the praise of Israel.
In you our fathers put their trust;
they trusted and you delivered them.
They cried to you and were saved;
in you they trusted and were not disappointed.
Psalm 22:3-5

In his arrogance the wicked man hunts down the weak, who are caught in the schemes he devises. He boasts of the cravings of his heart; he blesses the greedy and reviles the LORD. In his pride the wicked does not seek him; in all his thoughts there is no room for God. His ways are always prosperous; he is haughty and your laws are far from him; he sneers at all his enemies. He says to himself, "Nothing will shake me; I'll always be happy and never have trouble." His mouth is full of curses and lies and threats; trouble and evil are under his tongue. He lies in wait near the villages; from ambush he murders the innocent, watching in secret for his victims. He lies in wait like a lion in cover; he catches the helpless and drags them off in his net. His victims are crushed, they collapse; they fall under his strength. He says to himself, "God has forgotten; he covers his face and never sees."

    Psalm 10:2-11

Haman's Prejudice

Esther 3:8
Then Haman said to King Xerxes, "There is a certain people..."

Haman's pride and prejudice knew no bounds. Speaking with King Xerxes, he deceitfully showed concern for the king's position by mentioning a 'certain' people in the kingdom who were disobedient and 'different.' Without disclosing who the 'certain' people were, he made a case around the threat which may come from them in the long run. He even went as far as to suggest, *"that it is not in the king's best interest to tolerate them."*

In a conniving and cunning way, wicked Haman went about his evil business. His hatred for Mordecai had escalated into a national mass murder plot. King Xerxes, who disposed of people for little or no reason himself, showed absolutely no interest as to who the 'certain' people were! Haman had known beforehand that the king would be easily won over and his air of confidence and superiority before the king won the day. He mentioned to the king that the customs of the 'certain' people were different from the nationals. Of course they were different! Weren't they Jews? A people, chosen by God, set apart for the fulfilment of His plans and purposes and who followed His laws and decrees. Even in exile, they continued to obey God's laws. They had been told by God, through the prophet Jeremiah, how they were to conduct themselves in the country of their captivity, prior to their going (Jeremiah 29:4-7.) It seems they were obedient to the laws of king and country and lived as good citizens. Haman had exaggerated the situation for his own benefit, as the king's advisors had previously done, concerning Vashti. The prejudice at that time was against women in general. Now, it is because of religious belief.

Throughout history, people have shown prejudice towards their fellow man for one reason or another. Usually, it begins in the heart of one person, who then subtly draws others into their way of thinking. Very soon, the prejudice develops into a situation where whole families, communities and indeed countries are divided and set in opposition to each other. Mistrust, suspicion and hatred are the order of the day and sadly, those who show prejudice cannot fully explain or give a sound reason as to why they are prejudiced in the first place! Lack of knowledge, fuelled by 'historical' tales, regarding those to whom the prejudice is directed, keeps people from crossing the great divide and reconciling with those whom they perceive as being a threat. Unfortunately, prejudice is a seed bed for hatred which, when nursed and nurtured, can often lead to persecution and even, murder.

It is no wonder that Haman is caught in the net of prejudice against God's people. His lack of knowledge about the true God of Heaven, his ancestral history and his own pride mixed with the desire for power and self-exaltation, has so gripped him that murder is his only agenda.

Let us therefore make every effort to do what leads to peace and mutual edification.
Romans 14:19

*Father God, forgive us if there are any seeds of prejudice in our own lives.
Set us free from the influence of those who perpetuate such thoughts and actions against others.
May we be like Jesus who crossed over all borders which separated man from man, nation from nation and religion from religion.
Let Your Peace, Grace and Mercy be our portion in all of our dealings with others and may we see everyone through Your eyes of love and selfless sacrifice.*

"You have heard that it was said, 'Love your neighbour and hate your enemy.' But I tell you: Love your enemies and pray for those who persecute you, that you may be sons of your Father in heaven.
He causes his sun to rise on the evil and the good, and sends rain on the righteous and the unrighteous. If you love those who love you, what reward will you get? Are not even the tax collectors doing that? And if you greet only your brothers, what are you doing more than others?
Do not even the pagans do that? Be perfect, therefore, as your heavenly Father is perfect."
      Matthew 5:43-48

Haman's Power

Esther 3:9
"If it pleases the king, let a decree be issued to destroy them..."

What a request? Haman had every confidence in the argument he had put forward and it is with cold, calculated boldness, he asks for the king's endorsement on the holocaust.

I can imagine Haman, all dressed up in his finery, sounding important and convincing, while the king sat half listening to all that was being said. I don't think it would be stretching things too far to suppose that King Xerxes had appointed Haman to take some of the strain without being in total charge. He had entrusted Haman with a position of authority and, as such, left him to get on with it. As far as the king was concerned, Haman had popped in for his signature on a piece of paper and the speech didn't really interest him in the slightest. Maybe he yawned and gestured with his hands for Haman to hurry up and just say what it was he wanted.

Reading in the Book of Genesis, God tells us that He made man in His own image and likeness. To take the life of another human being is murder and the penalty for murder is death.

The sentence of death came upon the convicted murderer when found guilty by those who had been given the authority to judge them. If there was no-one convicted of the crime, then, it would seem, the criminal got away with their evil deed. What we need to remember is, that God, in His justice, will one day hold to account those who are guilty of such a crime and death in this case, will be separation from Him forever! The guilty one will not go free and the punishment will be eternal damnation!

King Xerxes had already sent to death many in his own household as well as others who disagreed with him or crossed him in any way. Murder was a lifestyle choice to this despot of a ruler and, as he sat, half listening to Haman as he spoke about a 'certain' people and then requested him to sign their death warrant, it was like a game to him. He probably reasoned that Haman needed to shed a bit of blood just to endorse his official status, so why not let him have his way. What we have here are two men who are void of conscience and unconcerned about the consequences of their actions, either on this earth or, beyond the grave.

It is gruesome reading and, as such, should drive us to our knees in prayer for those outside of Christ.

Father God, when we consider the conversation which took place that day so long ago, we are ever mindful of the fact that there are those who, even at this very moment, are plotting murder. We pray to-day that their evil intentions will fail. We would also pray that the Gospel of Jesus Christ would be delivered unto them.
We pray that their hearts would turn away from wickedness and sin and that they would repent and look to Jesus for forgiveness. That they would see the One who willingly shed His own blood on Calvary's cross in order that they would be set free from sin and the penalty of eternal death and seperation.
We pray this in Jesus Name.
Amen.

For the wages of sin is death, but the gift of God is eternal life in Christ Jesus our Lord.
Romans 6:23

Can a corrupt throne be allied with you - one that brings on misery by its decrees? They band together against the righteous and condemn the innocent to death. But the L ORD has become my fortress, and my God the rock in whom I take refuge. He will repay them for their wickedness; the L ORD our God will destroy them.
     Psalm 94:20-23

Haman's Promise

Esther 3:9
"I will put ten thousand talents of silver..."

When Haman came to the end of his speech, he added a further incentive in order to win over the king's consent, by promising to put into the royal treasury, ten thousand talents of silver as payment for the men who would 'carry out this business'. Either Haman was a very rich man, or his promise could only be endorsed after he had murdered all the Jews in the kingdom, and, taken their property and goods as plunder. Haman had put four arguments forward in presenting his case to the king;
"There is a certain people."
"They do not obey the king's law."
"It is not in the king's interest to tolerate them."
"A payment of ten thousand talents of silver would go to the royal treasury...."

They say, "money talks," and Haman would have known that the king had lost much in recent years through defeat in war. Tickling his senses with such a promise, not only showed Haman's subtlety while, at the same time, appealing to the king's battered ego. Surely purging those who did not honour and obey him, would make King Xerxes look powerful in the eyes of his enemies and give him some credibility once more!

In this instance, though, the king refused the money and told Haman to keep it. If he had not been a rich man before this, Haman would certainly become one in eleven months' time!

I am reminded of those times in Scripture when people were sold because of the jealousy, hatred and intolerance of others. Joseph is just one example, whose murder by his own brothers was their first consideration, but was then sold instead for twenty shekels of silver and taken to Egypt as a slave. To be hated by an enemy is one thing, but, to be hated and despised by those in whose company you have lived day by day is something else indeed. Sharing a meal, a walk, a conversation, either, within the family or circle of friends, is very precious. The sad part is, when we later discover that during those times, their intentions towards us were not good.

David expressed these same feelings, *"If an enemy were insulting me, I could endure it; if a foe were raising himself against me, I could hide from him. But it is you, a man like myself, my companion, my close friend, with whom I once enjoyed sweet fellowship as we walked with the throng at the house of God."* (Psalm 55:12-14)

Gracious Father, forgive us if there has ever been a time in our own lives when we have 'sold' someone because of jealousy, pride or by nursing a grudge.

We may not have received, or parted with actual money, but have perhaps arranged circumstances in such a way, as to cause separation, hurt or fear in someone else's life.

Help us to pray for, and have compassion towards those who are hurting to-day, because of the betrayal of others in whom they had placed their trust.

May we be reminded of Jesus, who 'knew from the beginning' the one who would betray Him, yet treated Judas as He did the others, right to the very end.

Give us the grace we need to live out His example with humility and fortitude.

*A good man obtains favour
from the* L<small>ORD</small>*,
but the* L<small>ORD</small> *condems a crafty man.
Proverbs 12:2*

A wise king winnows out the wicked;
he drives the threshing wheel over them.
Proverbs 20:26

Haman's Pleasure

Esther 3:10
So the king took his signet ring from his finger and gave it to Haman...

Through the inspiration of the Holy Spirit, the writer of the book of Esther reminds us, at this juncture, of who Haman is, *'... Haman son of Hammedatha, the Agagite,'* but then, added to this, are these words, **'the enemy of the Jews.'** Earlier we read of Mordecai, *'the Jew'* and now, we read of Haman, **'the enemy of the Jews.'** It is as if God wants us to know exactly who this person *really* is. The gauntlet has been thrown down. Let the battle commence!

Once again, and in true fashion, King Xerxes gives approval with no questions asked. Not only so, but without giving any thought to the outcome, the king takes off his signet ring and hands it over to Haman and the symbol of authority, which was afforded to the king alone, now, belongs to him! Whatever he may have expected by approaching the king in the first instance, Haman would not have thought that control of the kingdom would also be part of the outcome! Through lies, deceit, cunning and manipulation, he has now secured for himself absolute control over his evil plot. Then, to hear the king say, *"and do with the people as you please,"* must have given him pleasure beyond anything he had ever experienced before. It was mission accomplished indeed! The weak willed king had once again fallen victim to those who knew him better than he knew himself and who preyed upon his foolishness for their own ends. The puppet king had succumbed to the smooth words of a man whose heart wasn't much different from his own, but, whose craftiness and cunning went unnoticed, because King Xerxes lacked the wisdom necessary in this particular situation.

After Solomon became king of Israel, the LORD appeared to him and said, *"Ask for whatever you want me to give to you,"* (2 Chronicles 1:7). Such an invitation would cause most of us to come up with an answer which would grant us power, wealth and prestige. Not for Solomon though, his request was not centred in these things. Of course he wanted to be a great leader, but not for selfish purposes, or to oppress the people under his rule. His request was for **wisdom** and **knowledge** to govern in a fashion which honoured God, and his father, David. His request was not only granted, but God also promised to give him wealth, riches and honour as well! (verses 10-12)

Heavenly Father, there are times when we too, lack wisdom and the result is, that we fail miserably when dealing with our own affairs. Your word exhorts us to ask You for wisdom and yet, we quite often fail to do this. Is it because it seems too simple? Do we not really believe we can obtain it?
Maybe we think we don't need it! Surely, the reward in asking will deepen our faith and strengthen our dependence upon You. Give us the grace we need to seek You in our decision making, so that the outcome will be for our good and Your glory. May Your wisdom be our portion as we journey through life and address the issues which arise in day to day living. May it direct us in the various roles we play, whether this be in the home, school, college, church or workplace. Help us to be the best we can be for the sake of others, so that they would be blessed as a result.

If any of you lacks wisdom, he should ask God, who gives generously to all without finding fault, and it will be given to him.
(James Ch.1:5)

This is what the LORD Almighty, the God of Israel, says to all those I carried into exile from Jerusalem to Babylon: 'Build houses and settle down; plant gardens and eat what they produce. Marry and have sons and daughters; find wives for your sons and give your daughters in marriage, so that they too may have sons and daughters. Increase in number there; do not decrease. Also, seek the peace and prosperity of the city to which I have carried you into exile. Pray to the LORD for it, because if it prospers, you too will prosper.'
     Jeremiah 29:4-7

Haman's 'certain' People

Zechariah 2:8
... for whoever touches you touches the apple of his eye.--

During the reign of King Nebuchadnezzar God sent His people into captivity for seventy years. Through the prophet Jeremiah, God gave them instructions as to how they should live. Reading the passage clearly shows, that God's people were not to be antagonistic towards their captors; rather, they were to, *'build; settle; plant; marry; increase in number and pray for the prosperity of the cities in which they lived.'* There is a strong indication here that they were to play a major role in the communities in which they would live, which, of course, would also add to the economic climate of the realm. The contribution the 'certain' people made throughout the kingdom of Persia would have been immense. Sadly, King Xerxes hadn't noticed, or if he had, surely, he would have argued this point with Haman. Furthermore, Haman was so caught up in hatred, pride, selfishness and murderous thoughts, that even he, had not given thought to the great loss this 'certain' people would have on the economy of the kingdom.

As promised, when seventy years were over, God gave opportunity for them to return to Israel, their homeland. Not all of the exiles did return however, and it is for this reason we now read of the 'certain' people in the book of Esther. Obviously they did, *'settle, build, plant, marry, prosper and pray.'* At least two generations were born in captivity and had never been to Israel, so, for those exiles, this was their home. Their livelihoods had been attained through hard work, diligence, prayer and obedience to God's commands. Having to leave all they had worked for and built up, was not what they wished to do. It seems, that among those who stayed behind, were the ancestors of Mordecai and Esther.

This 'certain' people were God's chosen people. It mattered not where they lived, He was still their God. His promises towards them would not and could not fail. He would keep His covenant with them as He had promised to Abraham. Although they had failed on their part to keep covenant on many occasions, God was still long suffering and merciful towards them. They were the *'Apple of His eye.'* and as such, nothing would befall them unless God caused it or allowed it. This was something Haman was yet to discover.

The New Testament calls the 'certain' people, 'peculiar' people. As such, nothing will befall us either, unless God causes, or allows it!

*Thank-you Father that we too,
are the 'apple of your eye' because our lives
are hid in Christ.
Like a mother hen protecting her chicks,
so You protect us.
Thank-you for Your promise of never leaving us
or forsaking us.
Thank-you that we can approach You
any time of the day or night.
Thank you that You hear us when we cry out to You.
Thank you for the hope we have of one day seeing
You face to face.
Thank you for the sure and certain hope
of eternal life.
Thank you that, even today, those things
which concern us, concern You.*

*..for whoever touches you,
touches the apple of his eye...
Zechariah 2:8*

They were the 'apple of God's eye.'
Divine love chose to hear their cry
And brought them out of slavery,
Through sin and shame and suffering,
Into the land He'd promised them.
But disobedience and sin
Spoiled their relationship with Him,
Scattered them from the promised land.
Divine love still holds out His hand.
God waits, in love, for their return,
His promises are sure and firm
To Israel, He will draw nigh.
They are 'the apple of God's eye.'
Divine love gave our Lord to die.
God gave 'the apple of His eye,'
His only Son to bear the guilt
Of all our sin upon Himself.
Love to the uttermost was given,
Grace was poured out on earth from heaven.
Christ died upon that awful cross
To save us all from sin and loss.
Abundant love! Abundant grace!
Some day we'll see Him face to face
And know, in full, the reason why
We are 'the apple of God's eye.'

Olive Gardiner

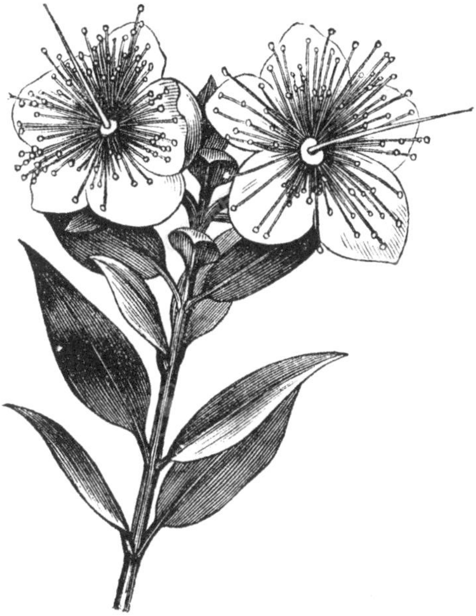

Bloodthirsty men hate a man of integrity and seek to kill the upright.
    Proverbs 29:10

Haman's Urgency

Esther 3:12
Then on the thirteenth day of the first month the royal secretaries were summoned.

The fourteenth day of the first month was Passover for the Jews. It was the day when they remembered the deliverance of their ancestors from Egypt. For the Hebrew child of God, it was a day of prayer, feasting and celebration. As the Hebrews, throughout the Persian Kingdom, prepared for this special day in their spiritual calendar, Haman was busy dictating the words of their death warrant! He wasted no time in summoning the royal secretaries, who wrote out in the language of each people, in each province, his evil instructions. Perhaps he thought the king would change his mind, so he made it a matter of urgency to have this part of the job done. On the other hand, he may have been delighting himself with the notion that all the Jews would be trembling in fear over the next eleven months! Relishing in this kind of power and control over others would only add to his blood-thirsty desires. Haman was on a roll and nothing would stop him from pursuing his evil intentions.

The orders were written in the name of King Xerxes, for all the governors, nobles and leaders of the provinces and were then sealed with the king's own signet ring.

Pressing the king's seal into the melted wax and then applying it to the scrolls, must have given Haman such a feeling of superiority. His pride, which had already been displayed by the order given to kneel down in his

presence, must now, be inflated even more.
He was in complete control!
His word was now law!

Yes, the edict may have had the king's name and seal attached to it, but for Haman that day, the words were his; the directive was his; the power was his, and the plan was his.

Heavenly Father.
How we long for evil in all its forms
to be put away forever.
We thank You that Jesus
conquered sin and
death on the cross
and that in Him,
there is victory over sin
and its power in our lives.
*We thank You that **Your Word**,*
which is the law of grace and truth,
*offers **life**,*
not only for now, but for eternity.
Thank you for the invitation to come
to Jesus, who alone,
has the power to forgive
all our sins
and iniquities.

*Jesus answered,
"I am the way
and the truth
and the life."
John 14:6*

The wrath of God is being revealed from heaven against all the godlessness and wickedness of men who suppress the truth by their wickedness. They have become filled with every kind of wickedness, evil, greed and depravity. They are full of envy, murder, strife, deceit, and malice. They are gossips, slanderers, God-haters, insolent, arrogant and boastful; they invent ways of doing evil; they disobey their parents; they are senseless, faithless, heartless, ruthless.
      Romans 1:18,29-31

Haman's Dispatch

Esther 3:15
Spurred on by the king's command, the couriers went out.

The 'Postal Service' consisted of riders who lined the roads throughout the kingdom of Persia and who, in their turn, carried the royal information from place to place. It proved to be a fast and effective way for Haman to have the king's edict delivered. Rubbing his hands with glee, Haman would have watched as the horsemen left Susa carrying the orders to; *'destroy, kill and annihilate all the Jews - young and old, women and little children - on a single day, the thirteenth day of the twelfth month, the month of Adar, and to plunder their goods.'* (3:13)

If this situation was happening to-day we could imagine Haman 'high-fiving' everyone he meets! Pride, prejudice and pleasure were the order of the day and he would have been on cloud nine! Haman knew that once the law was written and sealed, it could not be changed. The fate of the Jews in the kingdom had at last been decided and the people of every nationality would now be aware of the death warrant which would hang over the heads of their Jewish neighbours for the next eleven months.

There was nowhere to hide!
They could not avoid the holocaust!
Their children would die also!
Their race would be wiped out!
Who could they turn to for help?

Away from Susa, people knew nothing of the conniving and scheming going on in the royal palace and, as the edict would be read out in public and posted on gates and hoardings throughout the kingdom, fear, apprehension and deep sorrow would grip everyone. We would not be making wrong assumptions in thinking, that even those who were not Jews, would also have been shocked to hear of the king's orders. There would be much confusion and dismay, as folk tried to comprehend the reason behind this awful edict which intended to bring about the complete annihilation of their neighbours, friends and working companions. They had seen, in the past how quickly people could be dispensed with when Vashti was removed as queen. The women of the Persian kingdom had suffered when they had been left open to all sorts of abuse towards them because of a previous edict, as a result of Vashti's disobedience. This time it was different; the bar had been raised to another level. This was an intended holocaust! Surely everyone would be at risk sooner or later, for some reason or another when, at the stroke of a pen and with the seal of a signet ring, anything was possible. There was no escape from anyone who wished to rear their evil head in order to oppress, dictate and suppress, once pride, selfishness and a thirst for power took them captive.

Create in me a pure heart, O God, and renew a steadfast spirit within me.
Psalm 51:10

Heavenly Father, help us to keep in mind that these were real people in real time, therefore, we have little or no idea what it must have felt like to read the king's edict as they did. Many times in history and even in this present day, such threats have been and are, being made and carried out, on particular sections of society. May we purge ourselves of any semblance of pride or prejudice. Search our hearts Lord and show us those areas which harbour any animosity for any reason, towards another fellow human being. Forgive us and cleanse us from any intolerance, racism or attitudes we have, which may cause fear, apprehension or sorrow in someone else. We pray for any who are suffering to-day at the hands of an oppressor, terrorist threat, or a tyrannical regime. May they know Your presence, strength, comfort and love.
In Jesus Name we pray.

"Wake up, O sleeper, rise from the dead, and Christ will shine on you."
Ephesians 5:14

Haman's Indifference

Esther 3:15
The king and Haman sat down to drink, but the city of Susa was bewildered.

As the people of Susa read the king's edict when it was posted around the city, they were totally bewildered. No-one could figure out the reason for such a notice. Why would a particular section of the community be targeted for death? What had happened that the king would want to carry out this holocaust? Question after question must have been aired in every house and street, as the people wondered and deliberated. Fear mixed with sorrow, would soon overcome them and, like the rest of the kingdom, folk might be thinking, *"who will be next!"*

Behind closed doors, Haman was distracting the king's attention from all that was happening outside the palace walls. In his cold, calculating manner, he was enjoying 'happy hour' in the king's company, while the citizens of Susa were in turmoil.

We have come to see that Haman was a very wicked and evil man. Therefore, it should be of no surprise to us to find him displaying such indifference, particularly, as he had been responsible for what was taking place. He was so filled with self-satisfaction and pride in the power he had just wielded across the kingdom and, in the king's name, that he felt he needed to celebrate his seeming victory. It didn't bother him one bit that the king was totally unaware of the extent to which he had gone with the authority given to him. After all, the king did say, *"and do with the people as you please."*

So, he did!

Haman's message of death and destruction, rose out of a heart filled with pride, prejudice and racism and now he had spread that message throughout the whole Persian kingdom.

It can be very easy for us to condemn and criticise Haman for his indifference towards a people who were facing the penalty of death, while at the same time, ignoring the indifference in our own lives.

We too, have a message, and that message is one of life, not only for now, but for eternity! It is a message of salvation, hope, peace, love and promise and sometimes I wonder if we do enough to spread it. While we rejoice in what God has done in our own lives, we need to remember, that there is a community around us which is facing eternal death. The wrath of God will one day fall and many of God's people are totally indifferent to the plight of those who do not know Christ and His offer of salvation. People are perishing while we languish over cups of tea and buns! There is nothing wrong with having fellowship one with another, the Bible exhorts us to do this, but we need to get the perspective right. We have to cultivate a passion for lost souls and get the gospel message out.

Haman will be held accountable for his evil deeds by a holy and righteous God one day. His indifference towards the death of innocents may deserve our contempt but his thoughts and actions should not negate *our* responsibility and leave us in a position whereby, we too will have to give an account for ***our indifference!***

Gracious God and Heavenly Father, give us such passion that will drive us to our knees, weeping and praying for souls which are lost.
Pour into our indifferent hearts, that same love, you have for them.
May we not be like the Pharisee and the Levite who passed by on the 'other side of the road,' leaving a wounded, bruised and dying man.
Give us the same heart of compassion the Samaritan showed, as he put aside pride, prejudice and racism and offered help and assistance to the same man.
Help us to pray for those on the 'other side' of our roads, tables and workbenches.
As we share the message of love, life and hope to the hurting, downcast, bruised and dying, give them the gift of faith to receive You into their lives and situations.
Help us to rise up out of our apathy and circulate the message Jesus commanded when He said,
"Go into all the world and preach the good news to all creation" Mark 16:15

God of the poor
Friend of the weak
Give us compassion we pray
Melt our cold hearts
Let tears fall like rain
Come change our love
From a spark to a flame

Lighten our darkness
Breathe on this flame
Until Your justice
Burns brightly again
Until the nations
Learn of Your ways
Seek Your salvation
And bring You praise.

Graham Kendrick

Payer and Praise

O LORD, do not rebuke me in your anger or discipline me in your wrath. Be merciful to me LORD, for I am faint; O LORD, heal me, for my bones are in agony. My soul is in anguish. How long, O LORD, how long? Turn, O LORD, and deliver me; save me because of your unfailing love. No-one remembers you when he is dead. Who praises you from his grave? I am worn out from my groaning; all night long I flood my bed with weeping and drench my couch with tears. My eyes grow weak with sorrow; they fail because of all my foes. Away from me, all you who do evil, for the LORD has heard my weeping. The LORD has heard my cry for mercy; the LORD accepts my prayer. All my enemies will be ashamed and dismayed; they will turn back in sudden disgrace.

Psalm 6

Mordecai's Grief

Esther 4:1
When Mordecai learned of all that had been done, he tore his clothes...

Mordecai's grief was intense. He now knew that it was Haman's intention to annihilate the whole Jewish race and his response to the news of the holocaust brought him to a place of complete despair and anguish;
He tore his clothes!
He put on sackcloth and ashes!
He went out into the city!
He wailed loudly and bitterly!

What a pitiful sight Mordecai must have been as he made his way to the king's gate, but, as no-one was allowed to enter beyond the gate when clothed in sackcloth, he could not go any further. Of course, he wasn't alone in his grief. We are told that in every province to which the edict and order of the king came, there was great mourning with fasting, weeping and wailing. We also learn, many lay in sackcloth and ashes, so, throughout the city of Susa, the situation would have been just the same. What dreadful scenes these must have been for the non-Jewish communities as they watched grown men weep in the streets; whole families, weeping and wailing; little children, not fully realizing what was happening, yet, very upset as they watched their elder brothers, sisters, parents and grandparents in such a state of utter despair. The whole thing must have been unbearable for everyone.

Mordecai would have realised that it was his refusal

to kneel down before Haman which had led to this reaction. There may have been moments when waves of guilt and responsibility swept over him as this came to mind. Standing up for what he thought was right, resulted in the whole Jewish race now having to face death and complete destruction! *"What can be done; what can be said; Who can help us; Where can we go?"* The people of Susa would have been screaming and crying out these questions. Mordecai needed to dig deep.

It would be of great comfort for him to remember the words of Isaiah the prophet, who wrote, *"In all their distress, He too was distressed..."* Isaiah 63:9

Heavenly Father, there are times when we
take a stand for what we believe is right but,
it can result in repercussions for others.
Help us not to become divided, rather,
endeavour to keep our fellowship intact.
Show us how to be strong together and to consider
Your Word in such circumstances.
Help us as we look to You to redeem the situation
so that that Your Name will be glorified.

You come to the help of those who gladly do right who remember Your ways.
Isaiah 64:5

"A new command I give you: Love one another. As I have loved you, so you must love one another. By this all men will know that you are my disciples, if you love one another."
   John 13:34,35

Mordecai Reported to Esther

Esther 4:4
When Esther's maids and eunuchs came and told her...

Within the confines of the palace, Esther was completely unaware of what was happening outside in the city. She had no idea that her cousin and Haman had been engaged in a battle of 'rights.' Haman demanding the 'right' that everyone kneel in his presence and Mordecai standing for his 'right' not to kneel to an *'enemy of the Jews.'* Nor would she have known that Haman had plotted the deaths of every Jew in the kingdom as a result of Mordecai's defiance! As the drama unfolded, her maids and eunuchs came to her and reported Mordecai's grief and of his wearing sackcloth and ashes. Esther's response to the news was one of great distress. She knew Mordecai must have a very good reason for such an expression of grief and it probably broke her own heart to learn that her beloved cousin and 'adoptive father' was so filled with anguish and despair and that her situation did not allow her to go to him and comfort him. How sad Esther must have felt and how she must have longed to have been with Mordecai at this time.

Mordecai was in the king's employ and his position meant he 'sat at the king's gate'. His job allowed him on occasions, to enter into the inner court. He knew he would not be allowed to wear sackcloth and ashes inside the gate, so perhaps he ventured thus far, so that word of what was happening would reach Esther. Knowing Mordecai could not come into the inner court dressed as he was and that she could not go outside the gate, Esther sent clothes for him to wear instead of the sackcloth, but, he would not accept them. Apart from that, for the last five years, she had kept her Jewish upbringing a secret as Mordecai had instructed. Her servants, though, seemed to be aware that she knew Mordecai and they may have known also, that she too, was Jewish. When Esther had first arrived at the palace, she found favour with everyone who came into contact with her and there is no reason to believe that had changed. It may have been that some of her attendants were Jewish themselves, or, that Esther's 'fragrant' attitude was still bringing a sense of refreshment into what would be an otherwise unpredictable and depressing place for them to work. If they had known she was a Jew, they too, had kept her secret from the king and Haman.

Blessed is he who has regard for the weak.
Psalm 41:1

*LORD there are times in our lives
when it is impossible
to be with those whom we love
when they are sad or grieving.
Our hearts break for them
as we seem powerless to help.
How we long to be with them and
comfort them in their hurt.
May they remember,
You are always present.
You never slumber or sleep.
You give songs in the night.
You watch over our coming and our going.
You took our sins and our sorrows
and made them Your very own.
O, Father, give them a real
sense of Your presence today.
Reveal Yourself to them
in Your Word.
Soothe their troubled souls
and give them the strength
to face the trial.
May You be everything
our loved one needs to-day.*

Be merciful to me, O God, for men hotly pursue me; all day long they press their attack. My slanderers pursue me all day long; many are attacking me in their pride. All day long they twist my words; they are always plotting to harm me. They conspire, they lurk, they watch my steps, eager to take my life.
      Psalm 56:1,2,5,6

Mordecai's Explanation and Request

Esther 4:7
Mordecai told him everything that had happened to him...

Esther could not understand why Mordecai had refused the clothing she had sent, so she ordered one of the king's eunuchs who attended her, to go and find out what the trouble was. Mordecai told Hathach the whole story of what had happened to him, including the exact amount of money Haman had promised to pay into the royal treasury for the destruction of the Jews. He also sent Esther a copy of the edict for their annihilation, which Haman had published throughout the kingdom. He asked Hathach to explain all this to Esther and told him to urge her to go into the king's presence to beg for mercy and plead with him for her people. Now she knows!

The situation was very serious indeed and considering the amount of money Haman had promised, the fate of the Jews was sealed.

Yet, Esther did not do as Mordecai asked!

She did not go into the king's presence!
She did not beg for mercy!
She did not plead for her people!

Instead, she sent a message back to Mordecai reminding him the law stated that anyone who went before the king without his invitation, would be put to death. Being queen did not exempt her from this law!

Her life would be in danger should she go to the king uninvited and, she added, the king had not asked for her in thirty days!

Having lived in the palace of King Xerxes for five years, Esther had come to learn that life in a palace was not what every little girl dreamt it might be! She may be queen, but she was still just 'another' amongst Xerxes' playthings.

At first, it seemed that Esther was unwilling to do anything Mordecai had asked of her. This would be an unusual occurrence, as we have already noted that Esther had honoured Mordecai by her obedience in other areas of her life. She probably couldn't understand Mordecai suggesting that she put her own life at risk, so she sent Hathach out to remind him of the law and that if anyone wished to have an audience with the king, there was a procedure to follow. Unfortunately, once the request was made to see the king, the eventual decision probably lay with Haman! Obviously, that was not an option in this situation and Esther most likely felt they were defeated before they even started. Like her cousin Mordecai, she was going to have to dig deep and recall what God had done for her people in the past when the enemy came and the problem looked insurmountable.

Was Esther refusing to act or was she being cautious? Mordecai will answer that!

Let us then approach the throne of grace with confidence, so that we may receive mercy and find grace to help us in our time of need.
Hebrews 4:16

King of Kings, how we thank You that we can approach Your Throne without ever having to request an audience.
We thank You that You are only too pleased to listen to Your royal sons and daughters.
Because of Jesus we are welcome, acceptable and precious.
The Law kept us apart but Grace has drawn us near.
Thank You that we no longer live in fear of death, or separation from You.
Thank You that in Jesus we live and move and have our being.

Now I want you to know, brothers, that what has happened to me has really served to advance the gospel. As a result, it has become clear throughout the whole palace guard and to everyone else that I am in chains for Christ. Because of my chains, most of the brothers in the Lord have been encouraged to speak the word of God more courageously and fearlessly.

      Philippians 1:12-14

Mordecai's Reaction

Esther 4:14
... And who knows but that you have come to royal position for such a time as this.

When Mordecai received Esther's message his reaction seems to have been one of anger and disappointment. He reminded his cousin that living in the king's house would not provide her with protection from Haman's evil plot. He also told her that to remain silent would not prevent relief and deliverance coming from another place.

What did Mordecai mean by this?

First of all, it shows us that he was a man who trusted in the promises of God and relied upon God's faithfulness to the covenant He had made with Abraham. Although God is not mentioned in the book, we are reading a story which is about His own chosen people who have stayed in the land of their captivity while others had returned to Israel.

Secondly, Mordecai was aware that God cared for, and protected, His people, no matter where they were living. That being the case, he suggested to Esther that if she didn't help, then God would raise up someone else! He was absolutely sure that God would come to the aid of His people, with or without Esther!

Even if his message to Esther contained tones of anger, Mordecai was making it clear, that she too, was included in the king's edict concerning the holocaust. Rather than remain silent regarding her true nationality, he was directing her to use her position of influence on behalf of God's people.

After all, Mordecai reasoned, Esther's being queen and therefore, having access to King Xerxes, might just be, *'for such a time as this.'* This then is Mordecai's message to Esther, in, what he sees as God having placed her in what may become their **House of Redemption.**

Paul the apostle when writing to the Philippians, saw his imprisonment as a victory, rather than a defeat. Those who had incarcerated him thought they had shut him up. On the contrary, Paul used his situation to be of influence for Christ. He went on to say, *"The important thing is that in every way...Christ is preached. And because of this, I rejoice."* He rejoiced in the knowledge that God was still being glorified and that he was at the very centre of God's will, even in imprisonment!

Often we grumble about our circumstances with phrases such as, *"I hate this school," "I hate this job," "I hate this neighbourhood," "I hate..."* I'm sure Paul 'hated' many things about his situation. His freedom had been taken away, his fellowship with other Christians had been limited, his ability to travel was non-existent. Many restrictions and deprivations ensued when his liberty was taken away. Yet, in all of this, Paul rejoiced because it most certainly ***did not shut him up!*** He was not silenced, nor did he choose silence. He testified of Jesus loud and clear; he wrote letters to the churches at Philippi and Ephesus; he continued to pray, read and encourage. He was not silenced. Paul may have been imprisoned by the king of Rome, but he was always about the King's (God's) business.

*Heavenly Father, may we see that in all
and every place we find ourselves,
it is always,
for such a time as this.
Hadassah (Myrtle,) had been planted
in the house of King Xerxes,
totally unaware that her being there
was for the redemption of Your people.
Like the apostle Paul,
cause us to rejoice,
rather than regret and
bemoan our circumstances.
Give us the grace to accept this
as the place of Your choosing.
Help us to embrace that truth
and to bloom
where You have planted us.*

> Therefore, there is now no condemnation for those who are in Christ Jesus, because through Christ Jesus the law of the Spirit of life set me free from the law of sin and death.
> Romans 8:1,2

Mordecai's Stirs Esther's Calling

Esther 4:13
... Do not think that because you are in the King's house, you alone of all the Jews will escape.

Esther had received the advice from Mordecai she was looking for. She had not done what he had asked beforehand as it would have been foolish to act in haste. She realised the situation was desperate and wisdom was needed in order for her to seek help from the king. Perhaps Mordecai had felt she had not been willing to help her people, but, by his reaction, he actually gave Esther the confidence she needed and the reminder of just who she really was!

She was a child of God!
She belonged to a chosen people!
She worshipped the living God!
She was in the place of influence for His purposes!

Esther had been stirred up by Mordecai's response.

She embraced the situation fully.
She committed herself to action.
She was prepared to die if necessary.
She grasped her destiny with both hands.

Haman may have condemned her to death, but the God of Israel was her strength and her confidence. Esther may have reminded herself, *"The LORD redeems his servants; no-one will be condemned who takes refuge in* him." (Psalm 34:22);

When writing to young Timothy, Paul wrote, *"For this reason I remind you to fan into flame the gift of God which is in you."* Paul was encouraging Timothy to 'stir up' what God had given him and called him to do. He went on to say, *"For God did not give us a spirit of timidity, but a spirit of power, of love, and of self-discipline."* (2 Timothy 1:6,7)

While Haman went about 'stirring up' wickedness and evil, Esther was being 'stirred' into Godly action by her cousin Mordecai. She was going to take her God given authority over this impending disaster, with power, love and self-discipline.

So, she sent another message to Mordecai...

LORD there are times we need the encouragement from fellow believers to stir us into action. To remind us of who we are in Christ and to point us to those scriptures which show us the authority we have from You. Help us be more aware of situations into which we can speak words of life and love.
Stir our hearts to hear the cries of others as they look for deliverance.
Guide us on the path of our destiny with Your wisdom and truth.
May we not become complacent, comfortable or aloof, from the problems around us.

Do not merely listen to the word, and so deceive yourselves. Do what it says.
James 1:22

> Therefore, I urge you brothers, in view of God's mercy, to offer your bodies as living sacrifices, holy and pleasing to God - this is your spiritual act of worship.
> Romans 12:1

Mordecai's Obeys the Queen

Esther 4:16
"I will go to the king, even though it is against the law. And if I perish, I perish."

Esther had made her decision and now it was time for all the Jews in Susa to support her. She commanded Mordecai to gather them all together and fast for her. He was to instruct them to fast for three days and nights, while she too, would fast along with her maids. When the three days were over, then, she would go before the king.

I'm sure when Mordecai heard this news, his heart skipped a beat. Little Esther, his lovely cousin, had not turned her back on her people! How elated he would have been, as he thought upon the providence of God in their lives. Esther had grown into a beautiful young woman and had surely, been set aside by God, *'for such a time as this.'* Esther, the orphan, now Queen of Persia, had been chosen before the foundation of the world, to be in the place of influence at just the right time. What a God! Not only that, He was a God of miracles; The God of his ancestors; The God of Abraham; The covenant God of Israel. No, Esther had not failed or disappointed him, but had risen to the challenge. Mordecai was most likely experiencing one of the proudest moments of his life. Not the kind of pride that Haman indulged in, but pride in his nationality and in his beloved Esther, who was now willing to risk her life; and most of all, pride in the God of Israel.

Mordecai would have wasted no time in gathering up the Jews of Susa. With renewed confidence mixed with trepidation, he would explain to them what Esther's intentions were and how much she now needed them to do their part. They were to fast, for three days and nights, before she would go to the king. Since reading Haman's awful death warrant, the Jewish men, women, and all who could understand, would, for a brief spell, breathe in an air of hope. Their spirits would have been lifted as they sensed that *something* was being done on their behalf. That *something* would be Esther's sacrificial act on behalf of her people.

First, though, they were to fast. Fasting also implies prayer being made. As they would spend the next three days and nights without food or water, they would be calling upon the God of Abraham to come to their aid, to protect their lovely Queen Esther, to overturn, in some way, the evil edict which Haman had issued in the king's name and so deliver them from this impending calamity.

Esther knew that what she was about to do, could not be done, unless, God was with her. Requesting the prayers of others was such a sensible decision and it also included them in the outcome, whatever that outcome might be.

Greater love has no-one than this, that he lay down his life for his friends.
John 15:13

*Gracious God, it is no small thing
to contemplate laying down
one's life for the salvation of others,
yet, this is what Jesus did for us.
He willingly went to the cross
on our behalf and carried out
Your will for mankind.
As we meditate upon
His sacrifice today,
may we be willing
to lay our all
on the altar for You.
Give us a fresh sense of
holiness, self-sacrifice,
and complete surrender.
In Jesus Name.*

Hear my prayer, O LORD, listen to my cry for help; be not deaf to my weeping.
    Psalm 39:12

Esther's Preparation

Esther 4:16
Go, gather together all the Jews who are in Susa, and fast for me.

Prayer is a mighty weapon for the man and woman of God. It is also a privilege; one we take too much for granted. I remember reading the biography of a female missionary who had returned to her home in the U.S. after she retired from her work abroad. Having spent a large part of her life on the mission field with no access to Christian literature, she was excited to be living so close to a Christian book store. She told of a day she went to buy a book in that store, and, how amazed she was at the many books there were on the subject of Prayer and Discipleship. Shelves and shelves were taken up with books on these two subjects.

During her time as a missionary she had witnessed the casting out of demons and healing of the sick. Her dependence for success in these activities, came about through prayer, fasting and the reading of God's word. Drawing upon these resources, and, by the power of the Holy Spirit, God did wonderful things. Now, back home, she was finding it difficult to understand why so many books were necessary on these subjects when God had already given Christians the ability to do His work, provided they sought Him through prayer, and daily obedience to His Word.

The gospels tell the story of a man who had a demon-possessed son. He had asked Jesus' disciples to cast it out and they could not. After Jesus had cast it out, the disciples asked Him why they hadn't been able to do so.

Jesus rebuked them for their lack of faith. The account in Mark's gospel tells us that Jesus also told them, *"This kind can come forth by nothing, but by prayer and fasting."*

The lesson Jesus was teaching his disciples was, that there is *power* in faith. But faith, even as small as a mustard seed, is only powerful when it has been cultivated in time spent with God. We cannot, and dare not, try to do anything in our own strength. We can only draw from His resources and stand in His authority because we have spent time in prayer and the study of His Word.

Nine of the disciples had been left by Jesus when He had taken Peter, James and John up onto the mountain where they had seen Him transfigured before them. Down in the valley, the disciples struggled to cast out the demon from the boy. They had lacked *power* because they had not spent time seeking God. Later on, in the Garden of Gethsemane, Jesus rebuked Peter for sleeping when he and the others should have been praying. He said to him, *"Watch and pray, so that you will not fall into temptation..."* Had Peter done so, he would have been spared the agony he caused himself when he denied the Lord. Faith is only faith after it has been tested. Peter realized that prayer, rather than sleep, would have given him victory in the test and not failure. He relied on his own strength and not on the Lord's.

His carelessness in prayer brought failure, not success.

Esther knew what was necessary for victory in the battle. Her first plan of action was to pray, fast and seek God's help before she would go to the king.

Having spent five years in the palace didn't quench her desire to go through with God. It seems obvious, in asking her maids to fast with her, she had been a good witness for God and that she had continued to practice her Jewish beliefs. Esther had gained the respect of those around her and time would tell whether or not her devotion would bring success for her and her people.

Gracious Father, as the daily grind consumes our time and energy and leaves little room for You, help us to get off the treadmill of life and step into Your presence more often.
May we take a fresh look at what we do and where we go, so that we can make space for prayer and study of the word.
Help us to de-clutter our lives, by removing those activities which are of no eternal benefit.
*Give us a fresh desire to serve You
in power and purpose.*
Teach us how to pray fervently.
*May we always be dependent upon Your ability and not our own,
to change the circumstances
for which we are praying.*

**The prayer of a righteous man
is powerful and effective.
James 5:16**

You are my King and my God, who decrees victories for Jacob. Through you we push back our enemies; through your name we trample our foes. I do not trust in my bow, my sword does not bring me victory; but you give us victory over our enemies, you put our adversaries to shame. In God we will make our boast all day long, and we will praise your name forever.

    Psalm 44:4-8

Esther Fasts

Esther 5:1
On the third day...

Regardless of the fact she was queen, Esther held no power whatsoever. She was also, only one, of a number of the many wives and concubines of the king. The king had not called for her for thirty days and she had no idea how he would respond to her sudden appearance. She was certain that death was imminent should the king not extend the gold sceptre to her, which would be an indication that he approved of her coming to him. Esther was in a catch twenty-two situation, because the edict Haman had drawn up had already condemned her to death. She had made the choice of committing the whole situation to God in prayer and she was now trusting that God would bring about the right ending to this awful story. Her days of prayer and fasting would have instilled in her the peace and promises of the God of her fathers. She knew she served the living God who was faithful to His people and so, she was about to step out in His strength, trusting wholly upon Him.

Three days of fasting wouldn't have done much for Esther's appearance, especially as she was planning to present herself before the throne of King Xerxes. When she had been brought to the palace several years previously in order to go before the king, it was necessary for her to have a whole year of special treatment! Esther had now spent three days praying and pleading with God on behalf of her people.

That would have been painful to say the least and, the intensity of prayer along with the fast, would surely be reflected in her lovely face.

Politically she had no influence.
Spiritually, she had everything heaven could afford!

It was now, the third day...

*Father we thank you for the place of prayer.
What a privilege it is to come before You and speak of those things which are heavy upon our
hearts and minds.
It is only in Your presence that we can find
peace and assurance.
We praise you that all the resources we need are
available from You.
Thank You that Your grace is sufficient
in all of our circumstances.
May we go in the strength and power
of Your promises.*

**Let the peace of Christ rule in your hearts.
Colossians 3:15**

*Do not be anxious about anything,
but in everything, by prayer and petition,
with thanksgiving,
present your requests to God.
And the peace of God,
which transcends all understanding,
will guard your hearts
and your minds
in Christ Jesus.
Philippians 4:6,7*

I delight greatly in the LORD; my soul rejoices in my God, For he has clothed me with garments of salvation and arrayed me in a robe of righteousness.
    Isaiah 61:10

Esther's Royal Robes

Esther 5:1
...Esther put on her royal robes and stood...

Esther and her maids had been wearing mourning clothes for the past three days as they prayed and fasted together. Now the third day had arrived! The praying had ended, the fasting was over, Esther had completed the first stage of the journey she would make to the inner court of king Xerxes. Outside the palace, all the Jews of the city of Susa were dressed in sackcloth and ashes, including Mordecai. Their clothing was an expression of deep grief which was seen by everyone around them. They would now be waiting patiently, to hear the outcome of Esther's approach to the king.

Esther would have risen early to prepare herself. She had prepared spiritually and now it was time to put faith into action. She needed to capture the king's attention, as she did when she first walked into his presence all those years ago. She laid aside her garments of grief and sorrow and put on her royal robes.

The picture of Esther reaching for the royal robes and putting them on, reminds me of an incident in my own life a few years ago while I was attending a conference. Before the second session of the day began, we stood to sing that beautiful song, 'King of Kings.' I had sung this before on many occasions, but that day it was different. As we sang the words, *'In royal robes, I don't deserve...'* my heart was touched in a very powerful way. I suddenly realised those words were meant for me, personally. Just then, I had a picture in my mind of Esther standing in her royal robes and in that moment, I saw myself!

I saw the sackcloth and ashes of my sin.
I saw how God dwelt in unapproachable light.
I saw how my sin excluded me from His presence.
I saw how the wages of my sin was death.

Then I had a vision of Jesus as He hung on the cross.
I saw Him hanging there for me!
His broken body draped in my filthy rags.
The garments of sin and shame.

I knew that I could not come before a Holy God wearing that condemning wardrobe, and, as I stood at the cross and mourned over my sin, in confession and humility of heart, His forgiveness was poured upon me. By His grace, mercy and love, I was now acceptable in God's sight, because;

> He exchanged *my* sackcloth and ashes,
> the garments of sin, shame and mourning,
> for *His* Robe of Righteousness.

I saw myself dressed, **'in Royal robes I don't deserve...'** and I began to weep...

That day, God gave me a fresh look at His grace and I have not been able to sing that song since, without it breaking my heart as I think upon the cross and what my Saviour did for me there. I cannot sing it without it causing me to be so thankful, that the King of Kings had extended to me, the gold sceptre, in the person of Jesus.

Esther knew that King Xerxes had a law which protected him from anyone approaching him unless they were invited to do so. The punishment for violating that law was death. To even come within the confines of the palace in sackcloth and ashes meant instant death also. Esther had been guilty on both these charges.

As she reached for her royal robes, the outward expression of who she was, and what her position was, she made her way to the inner court of the most powerful man in the world.

Would the sight of Queen Esther, arriving unannounced, uninvited, and dressed in the symbol of her status, be enough to capture the king's attention, in order for him to extend the gold sceptre?

Gracious Father, I thank you for giving me Jesus.
The only One who could ever pay the price of my sin.
I praise Your Name for clothing me
in His righteousness.
I praise You that I can stand in Your Presence
without judgment
or condemnation
because of Him.
Thank you for His robes, which, in Your sight,
are the outward and inward expression
of who I am and what my position is
in Christ Jesus.
Amen!

God made him who had no sin
to be sin for us,
so that in him we might become
the righteousness of God.
2 Corinthians 5:21

My feet stand on level ground; in the great assembly I will praise the LORD.
   Psalm 26:12

Esther goes to the King

Esther 4:16
"And if I perish, I perish"

The ruins of Persepolis which is a UNESCO world heritage site, give us some indication of what Esther faced that day. This would have been the summer residence of King Xerxes. Built by his father Darius 1 in 518 B.C., the site of the audience hall is very well preserved and is similar to the one which was at the palace of Susa. There were six rows of tall pillars leading to a raised area which is at the far end, over seventy-six metres away. This is where the king would have sat on the gold covered throne. He would have looked magnificent sitting there holding the gold sceptre which was the symbol of his power. Anyone who had ever been granted an audience with him would have felt very subdued and frightened in these surroundings.

Esther made her way to the inner court of the king. No-one stood in her way to prevent her from approaching him. The past three days of fasting, praying and pleading may have caused weakness in Esther physically, but her strength was found in the God to whom she had prayed and committed the situation. With grace, elegance and an inner confidence, she was a woman on a mission. For the first time in her young life, she was being tested in a way she had never experienced before. It would have been beyond her imagination to ever think that she was the one who would be chosen to put her life at risk for the sake of a whole nation. The task upon her shoulders was enormous and Esther would need to handle the whole situation with great wisdom.

As she stood in the distance, the king looked up and saw her. Perhaps with a slight gasp, Esther would have immediately fixed her eyes on the gold sceptre, which he held in his hand. Would God step in and save her from certain death? Would the past three days count for anything? Will help come for the people of God? Esther's heart may have skipped a beat or two in those waiting moments.

As King Xerxes looked at her he was pleased. Her slender form and lovely features had won his heart once more.

She waited and watched...

Then, he held out the gold sceptre that was in his hand and bade her to come forward.

As Esther made her way towards him, she was probably thanking God with every step she took. The sight of the gold sceptre inviting her into the presence of the king was indeed an answer to her prayers, the prayers of Mordecai, and, the prayers of the people of Susa.

As she walked the length of that great hall, with the king watching her every move, Esther needed to keep reminding herself why she was there.

Finally, she approached the throne and touched the tip of the gold sceptre!

The first part of her mission was now complete. Her life had been spared. It was crucial now for her to follow the leading of God, as she would speak to the king on her own behalf and, on behalf of her people.

> ***Your throne, O God,***
> ***will last forever and ever,***
> ***and righteousness will be***
> ***the sceptre of your kingdom.***
> ***Hebrews 1:7***

Heavenly Father, We stand in awe of Esther and her sacrificial efforts on behalf of a whole nation. This young woman knew that the future of the Jews lay entirely in Your hands. We thank-you for the faith she displayed and the example she has left us. Her fervent prayers brought her favour with the highest authority in the land. Thank-you that You are a prayer hearing and prayer answering God. May we be challenged and motivated to spend more time in prayer so that we become less and you become more.

Trust in the LORD with all your heart and lean not on your own understanding; in all your ways acknowledge him and he will make your paths straight.
       Proverbs 3:5,6

Esther's Invitation

Esther 5:4
"If it pleases the king…"

The king was anxious to know why Esther had come to see him. He must have known that it was something of great importance in order for her to take such a risk in coming uninvited. Having to make an appointment to see him meant that the king only dealt with those things which boosted his ego, or anything which may have added to his vast wealth and status. His gracious tone and generous offer to Esther probably astounded her;

"What is it, Queen Esther? What is your request? Even up to half the kingdom, it will be given you." (5:3)

The king's offer to her shows just how much he favoured her above all others. He was willing to give her wealth and position without even knowing what she wanted! Of course, we have already read of the king's impulsiveness in the past, and Esther was not so taken with the prospect of being a wealthy woman, that she would abandon the task before her. She was wise and had not come without praying and seeking guidance from God regarding the approach she should take. She had no intention either, of rushing headlong into a discussion about the Jews of the kingdom. That would have brought up Haman's name and she might be seen as being critical of him. After all, the king was very fond of Haman and had given him promotion and status. By showing any animosity towards him, Esther might not even get to the point of her request!

There was too much at stake and it would have revealed her own secret. No, this was not the right time to give the king an answer.

Very astutely, Esther responds instead with an invitation, *"If it pleases the king, let the king, together with Haman, come today to a banquet I have prepared for him." (5:4)*

She knew she needed to win the king over and the best way to start, was by allowing him to indulge in some of his own pleasures. He was always one for a party, and today was just as good as any. *"Why not?"* he thought to himself, and he quickly sent for Haman, *"So that we may do what Esther asks." (5:5)*

The king would normally be the one directing the course of the conversation during an audience. He would have also determined the outcome as he listened to various people in his presence. Yet here, we find him following Esther's lead! She is the one in charge! Just a few moments ago she had risked her life, and now, she has the king and Haman coming to a banquet!

She herself had not eaten or drunk anything for the past three days. Her cousin Mordecai and the Jews of Susa had also gone without food or drink. Now, there's a banquet arranged, a time which is usually one of feasting, fun and laughter, but while the king and Haman would be having a jolly old time, Esther would be waiting for just the right moment, to make her request to the king.

LORD, how we rejoice, as we see You at work on behalf of Your chosen ones.
We praise You that You have a plan for Your people.
We thank you that You can turn even the heart of a king in order that Your plan succeeds.
May we embrace the plan You have for our individual lives, whatever the sacrifice.

"For I know the plans I have for you,"
*declares the L*ORD*.*
Jeremiah 29:11

Obey the king's command, I say, because you took an oath before God. Do not be in a hurry to leave the king's presence. Do not stand up for a bad cause, for he will do whatever he pleases. Since a king's word is supreme, who can say to him, "What are you doing?" Whoever obeys his command will come to no harm, and the wise heart will know the proper time and procedure. For there is a proper time and procedure for every matter though a man's misery weighs heavily upon him.

      Ecclesiastes 8:2-6

Esther's Banquet

Esther 5:5
So the king and Haman went to the banquet Esther had prepared.

This was a very private party. Esther had invited only two guests, her husband the king, and his prime-minister, Haman. The two most important people in the Persian kingdom had now been placed in the hands of Esther. God had controlled the events in such a way, that Esther, in her obedience to Him, was now playing the lead role on this stage. Haman was certain that he was of such importance, only the king could upstage him. Even in this, he had wormed his way into the king's affections to such an extent, that he had already usurped the king's authority. He still held the signet ring which could effectively seal by law anything he felt needed to be suppressed, or which opposed his position. He was a very dangerous and cunning man indeed. However, Esther doesn't seem to have shown any sign of being intimidated by his being there. She was determined in spirit and purpose and was very much in control of all that was happening. The puppet king who had been manipulated on so many occasions in the past, might soon discover his right hand man had also used him for his own evil deeds. Haman, who was sitting opposite her, was not only licking his lips because of the food placed before him, but also, at the thought of the Jews, Esther's own people, being put to death and all their goods being plundered.

The orphaned cousin of Mordecai, under the mighty hand of God, was quietly and serenely waiting for the appropriate time to act. She knew she didn't need to rush, the death penalty issued by Haman was still ten months away. Patience and wisdom were necessary now.

The king was still curious though, to know Esther's reason for coming to him. He again asked Esther to make known her petition, promising her once more, up to half the kingdom. It seems that she was about to tell him, *"My petition and my request is this,"* at which point he probably perched himself on the edge of his seat, when, she asked for them both to return the next day for another banquet! *"....Then I will answer the king's question."* Esther was risking a lot by holding back an answer for a second time, especially when the king was slightly inebriated. Amazingly, he didn't lose his temper and demand an answer there and then. He could have forced Esther to make her request, instead, he decided to play her little game. So, both the king and Haman left Esther's banquet, looking forward to another one the next day, when the king would know the real reason as to why Esther had risked her life in approaching him uninvited.

For who has known the mind of the Lord that he may instruct him?
But we have the mind of Christ.
1 Corinthians 2:16

*Heavenly Father, we see in Esther
a confidence and boldness
only You can give in such circumstances.
As she laid her request before You
with prayer and fasting,
You imparted to her the wisdom, patience,
courage and tenacity necessary
for the task ahead.
Help us to remember the resources
we have available to us
who are in Christ,
so that together with You,
Your work in the world will continue
with good effect.*

Then the LORD replied: "Write down the revelation and make it plain on tablets so that a herald may run with it. For the revelation awaits an appointed time; it speaks of the end and will not prove false. Though it linger, wait for it; it will certainly come and will not delay. See, he is puffed up; his desires are not upright - but the righteous will live by his faith - indeed, wine betrays him; he is arrogant and never at rest. Because he is as greedy as the grave and like death is never satisfied, he gathers to himself all the nations and takes captive all the peoples.

    Habakkuk 2:2-5

Haman Boasts

Esther 5:10
Calling together his friends and Zeresh, his wife, Haman boasted to them...

Haman left Esther's banquet that day more pompous and proud than ever before. He was beside himself with excitement at the thought of having been invited by Queen Esther to another banquet the next day! He couldn't wait to get home and tell all that had happened. He called together his friends and family and strutted around boasting about his great wealth, his many sons, his honour and position. The icing on the cake, of course, was that he was the *only* person invited to accompany the king to Esther's banquet. Now that was a real feather in his cap, because it meant that he had access to a private conversation. The king wanted to know Esther's reason for coming to him and Haman was going to be there to hear it! I can imagine him strutting about like a prize peacock, arrogantly listing all his qualities as he sought the praise of those in his household. He was possessed by his self-importance and his thirst for power and prestige. Haman's motto could have been, "it's all about me." There was one thing which he could not boast about. He could not say *everyone* knelt before him, because Mordecai, even with the threat of death facing him, still refused to kneel. This was like salt in a wound for Haman. Even as he came away from the queen's banquet, *'happy and in high spirits,'* he observed that Mordecai *'neither rose nor showed fear in his presence'* and his rage, once again, flared (5:9).

While at home, as he boasted, Haman suddenly eclaimed, *"But all this gives me no satisfaction as long as I see that Jew Mordecai sitting at the king's gate," (5:13).*

Mordecai was the only one who could take Haman down from his throne of self-importance and he did not like it one little bit! His boasting before his friends and family was cut short because of Mordecai's behaviour and he couldn't even enjoy his moment of glory when he thought of him. Haman's hatred for one person escalated to a point whereby a whole nation was now under a death penalty! Such hatred is referred to in the Bible as, malice. We are commanded to get rid of it, because, Paul says, it grieves the Holy Spirit (Eph.4:32.) Malice is also likened to yeast. Yeast, even a very small amount, can soon spread throughout the loaf, consuming it and causing it to increase in size. Our lives would be like that of Haman's if we followed his example, because malice would not allow us to tolerate our 'Mordecai's' either! There are those who irritate us, whether it be at home, work, school, college or even, Church. If we do not put away the feelings which surface, we are not walking in the light of God. Other people's attitudes towards us, should not cause us to allow grievances or jealousies to fester and grow into malice. We need to ask God for the grace necessary in the situation if we are genuinely desiring to live in harmony with others.

*Heavenly Father, may we honour Your Name
in everything we do and say.
Forgive us for those times when we have allowed our feelings to rule over us.
Give us the grace we need as we learn how to handle the difficult people in our lives.
May we remember we are the temple of the Holy Spirit and that we need to get rid of wrong attitudes and anything which hinders Your work in our lives.
May we seek peace instead of discord.*

*Don't you know that a little yeast works through
the whole batch of dough?
Get rid of the old yeast that you may be a new
batch without yeast - as you really are.
For Christ our passover lamb,
has been sacrificed.
Therefore let us keep the festival,
not with the old yeast,
the yeast of malice and wickedness,
but with bread without yeast,
the bread of sincerity and truth.
1 Corinthians 5:6-8*

The LORD'S curse is on the house of the wicked, but he blesses the home of the righteous. He mocks proud mockers but gives grace to the humble. The wise inherit honour, but fools he holds up to shame.
        Proverbs 3:33-35

Haman's Delight

Esther 5:14
"Have a gallows built..."

When Haman disclosed his dissatisfaction over Mordecai, his wife Zeresh and all his friends had a suggestion. They told him to build a gallows seventy-five feet high and go and ask the king for permission to have Mordecai hanged on it. They encouraged him to then go and enjoy the banquet with Esther and the king. Sadly, even his own wife knew what would please Haman and she, along with the others knew his peace only lay in Mordecai's death. It would be very easy for him to gather up some reason or another for the king to sanction Mordecai's punishment.

This suggestion delighted Haman and, he had the gallows built.

Zeresh is one of those women in Scripture who will say or do anything to please her husband. She is just as twisted as he is. She probably had never even met Mordecai and yet on her husband's say so, this man was a thorn in his side and needed to be dealt with. Haman had already taken steps to do that, but his plan included the destruction of all the Jews of the kingdom. Zeresh thought the best way to deal with Mordecai was to get rid of him and to do it now. It amazes me to think that a woman who was the mother of ten sons could conceive such an idea. Obviously the influence of Haman in his own home had an effect on his wife and her opinions.

She reminds me of Herodias, wife of Herod, who nursed a grudge against John the Baptist and wanted to have him killed. She took the opportunity to do this at her husband's birthday party! During it, she allowed her teenage daughter to dance before Herod. He was pleased with her performance but under the influence of alcohol, he foolishly promised to give her anything she wanted, even up to half the kingdom. Not being able to make a decision just then, the girl went and asked for her mother's advice. Herodias took advantage of her daughter's situation and sent her back into Herod with a request. The girl approached Herod and asked for the head of John the Baptist! Not wanting to lose face before his distinguished guests, or to be seen to break his promise, Herod immediately sent the executioner to the prison. He quickly returned with John's head on a platter. He handed it to the girl, who, in turn, handed it to her mother. (Mark 6:14-29)

What a gruesome story this is! How could any mother do such a thing, we ask ourselves? The answer, they can and they do. When the yeast of malice spreads in the heart and consumes the mind, it must have an expression. It cannot be contained. With Herodias, it was expressed by requesting the head of John the Baptist. With Zeresh, it was the suggestion to hang Mordecai on a gallows seventy-five feet high.

A wife of noble character who can find?
She is worth far more than rubies.
Proverbs 31:11

*Gracious Father, our hearts desire is that our homes
would be a place of peace and love.
That our children would be pleasing in Your sight.
That they would follow after You and walk
in Your ways.
That we would be good examples of truth
and righteousness.
That we would be women who would be a blessing to
those around us.
That we would pass on the mantle of grace and love
to the next generation.
May our lives, therefore, display the fruit of the Spirit
in all we do.*

Arise, O LORD, in your anger; rise up against the rage of my enemies. Awake, my God; decree justice. Let the assembled peoples gather round you. Rule over them from on high; let the LORD judge the peoples. Judge me, O LORD, according to my righteousness, according to my integrity, O Most High. O righteous God, who searches the minds and hearts, bring to an end the violence of the wicked and make the righteous secure.
     Psalm 7:6-9

The King's Insomnia

Esther 6:1
That night the king could not sleep...

King Xerxes had difficulty sleeping after Esther's banquet. Perhaps he ate too much, or drank too much. Maybe he was wondering what could possibly cause Esther to be so bold, as to enter the inner court uninvited. I believe that God kept him from sleeping.

We have already noted the absence of any mention of God in this story, but, we cannot fail to notice His work behind the scenes. He *is* there, *all* the time, ordering events, situations, and people. Now, He causes the king to get up out of his bed and call for one of his attendants. He asked that the record of his reign be brought and read to him. As he listened, he heard of the account regarding Bigthana and Teresh, two of his officers who had guarded the doorway, and how their planned assassination attempt on the king had been exposed by Mordecai. His name had been recorded as the one who had saved the king from those who had been behind the plot.

Years had passed since that event was recorded and many other events in the king's reign had been recorded since then. How amazing it is, that on this particular night, the LORD brought this event to the king's attention! As he listened, he asked if Mordecai had received any reward for reporting this incident. The answer of course was, *"no."* The king wanted to acknowledge Mordecai's loyalty straight away. Mordecai should have been rewarded and the king was going to see that he was. No more delay on this matter, he wanted to sort it right then and there. It was still very early in the morning and the palace was quiet but the king was looking for someone to carry out his wishes, so, he asked if there was anybody in the court.

His attendant replied, *"Haman is standing in the court."*

Haman had no idea that he had walked on to centre stage, and was standing, not only in the king's court in the palace of Susa but also in the court of the King of kings, and, in the light of His penetrating gaze and anger.

It doesn't seem to be the case that Mordecai sought any reward even though he could have been greatly rewarded or promoted. He may have forgotten about the incident of the assassination plot as the years rolled by and he just got on with his job. There are times though, when no-one seems to notice the help we have given, or the effort we have put in. Years can pass, as we have seen, and it can cause us to feel discouraged and disappointed. We know that we should not be looking for any reward but, it can hurt when we seem to be ignored, while others are shown appreciation. It is always good to remind ourselves, that God never forgets.

He will remember and, *In His time* and, *in His unique way, He will reward us* accordingly. Mordecai is about to receive great honour and reward - God's way!

Whatever you do, work at it with all your heart, as working for the Lord, not for men.
Colossians 3:23

*Father God, thank you that our deeds
are recorded in Your book
and nothing will ever go unnoticed by You.
Help us to do those things
which will be of eternal value.
May we not seek the reward
or recognition of man
but live to serve and please You
in all that we do.*

He who is pregnant with evil and conceives trouble gives birth to disillusionment. He who digs a hole and scoops it out falls into the pit he has made. The trouble he causes recoils on himself; his violence comes down on his own head.
      Psalm 7:14-16

Haman's Horror

Esther 6:4
Now Haman had just entered the outer court of the palace...

Only God could write the script for what happened next!

Haman had arrived very early that morning to make sure he secured Mordecai's execution before he would go to Esther's banquet. He was looking forward to having a lovely time in the presence of the king and queen. The problem with Mordecai would be solved and he could relax and enjoy himself. As he entered the inner court, he heard the king's attendant call him. Thinking he was about to be given yet another accolade, he stepped into the presence of the king who had a question for him, *"What should be done for the man the king delights to honour?" (6:6.)* Without even asking who was to be honoured or what they were to be honoured for, so that he could decide what kind of reward was suitable, Haman thought, *"Who is there that the king would rather honour than me?"* There is just no end to Haman's pride!

The Bible says, *'God opposes the proud.'*

Unfortunately, Haman wasn't reckoning on that, as he gave his answer,

*"For the man the king delights to honour,
have them bring,
a royal robe the king has worn,
a horse the king has ridden,
one with a royal crest placed on its head.*

> *Then let the robe and the horse*
> *be entrusted to one of the king's most noble princes.*
> *Let them robe the man the king delights to honour,*
> *and lead him on the horse through the city streets,*
> *proclaiming before him,*
> *'This is what is done for the man the king*
> *delights to honour.'" (6:7-9)*

The king was very impressed with Haman's suggestion and as he waited for the king's response it is easy to imagine him square his proud shoulders, lift his chin in the air, and listen for the king as he called the attendants, who would then escort him off to receive his honour!

Haman was shocked when the king spoke, he did not hear his own name mentioned, instead, he heard Mordecai's name!

"Go at once," the king commanded Haman. *"Get the robe and the horse and do just as you have suggested for Mordecai the Jew, who sits at the king's gate. Do not neglect anything you have recommended." (6:10)*

The tables have begun to turn on wicked Haman. Here stands a man who has defiantly shaken his fist at God and his prideful, arrogant, self, imagines he is on winning ground. Haman, like so many, will soon realize that God wins *every* battle, *every* time, *all the time*.

He left the king's chambers to do for Mordecai, what he thought would have been happening to himself and he was absolutely mortified!

> **I waited patiently for the LORD;**
> **he turned to me and heard my cry.**
> **Psalm 40:1**

*Heavenly Father, only You could bring about
such a turn of events.
Sometimes we think you
are slow in coming to our aid
when we cry out to You.
Forgive us for our lack of faith.
We thank You that we are not left helpless.
You are watching
and noting those
who are persecuting us
and causing us grief.
One day You will repay them
for their sins against us.
Forgive us for our lack of patience
while we wait upon You.
Teach us how to be still
and know You are God.*

The eyes of the arrogant man will be humbled and the pride of men brought low; the LORD alone will be exalted in that day. The LORD Almighty has a day in store for all the proud and lofty, for all that is exalted (and they will be humbled). The arrogance of man will be brought low and the pride of men humbled; the LORD alone will be exalted in that day.
      Isaiah 2:11,12,17

Haman's Humiliation

Esther 6:11
So Haman got the robe and the horse...

Haman was ordered by the King to do for Mordecai what he had just suggested. He had to dress Mordecai in the king's robe, help him unto the horse and then lead him round the city calling out to everyone to pay respect to the man the king wished to honour. What a pitiful sight Haman must have been as he walked around the city leading the king's horse with Mordecai the Jew sitting on it! How his fortunes had been reversed. He probably hadn't slept a wink the night before thinking about Mordecai hanging from the gallows he had built and now, he was reduced to this! Haman must have wished for the ground to open up and swallow him. The Jews of Susa may have been wondering why this was happening, as they watched Mordecai riding on the king's horse, wearing the king's robe while they were still in sackcloth and ashes, mourning over their impending doom. This must have seemed a strange sight indeed. Perhaps the word began to circulate as to why Mordecai was being honoured in such a fashion, and, who it was who suggested it! That being the case, it probably brought some light relief into their otherwise grief-stricken situation, hearing the tables were turned on Haman.

Wicked, evil, Haman had wormed his way into a place of authority in the palace of King Xerxes. He had used manipulation, deceit, lies and cunning so that he could further his drive and passion for power. His next step was most likely, the throne itself. After all, why would he suggest such an extravagant reward for the man the king wanted to honour. Who else would wish to ride the king's horse, dress in the king's clothes and parade proudly round the city proclaiming his position, except, someone who had desired to be king?

Every time Haman had walked through the palace courts and then out into the streets, the people, great and small, had knelt before him.

Not today!

Today, they were kneeling before Mordecai the Jew. The very one who would not kneel before Haman. How utterly humiliated he must have felt.

Afterwards Mordecai returned to the king's gate. He had not forgotten that his people were still under a death threat.

As we read of the king's insomnia; the books he chose to have read to him; the account of Mordecai; the delay in rewarding him; Haman's early arrival, it reveals to us an awesome God. One who is Sovereign, all powerful, just and faithful. May we bring to Him to-day, those things which are causing us pain, hurt, stress, worry, fear or sadness, trusting in His unfailing power and ability to bring about the outcome which will be for our good and His glory.

Father, we thank You to-day for your love, care and protection.
We praise You for Your faithfulness.
We thank You that You are our Shield and our Defender.
We thank You that You have spread a table before us in the presence of our enemies.
We rejoice in the knowledge that You vindicate Your people.

*Who can proclaim the mighty acts of the L*ORD
or fully declare his praise?
Psalm 106:2

The LORD detests all the proud of heart. Be sure of this: They will not go unpunished.
    Proverbs 16:5

Haman's Downfall

Esther 6:12
But Haman rushed home, with his head covered, in grief.

This had been the worst day of Haman's life and the thought of going to Esther's banquet was far from his mind as he rushed home to tell his wife and all his friends everything that had happened to him.

The Bible tells us, he covered his head in grief. That is what Mordecai and all the Jews had done when they had first heard of Haman's evil edict to have them murdered. Yet again, the tables are turned and all Haman wanted to do was make it home and hide! He didn't know how he was ever going to appear in public again. Everyone would be laughing at him and teasing him. When he told his wife and his advisors the story, their response was amazing. They said,

"Since Mordecai, before whom your downfall has started, is of Jewish origin, you cannot stand against him - you will surely come to ruin!" (6:13)

What a statement! This time when he returned home, there was no boasting and strutting about, and, there was no-one stroking Haman's ego. Instead, it was his wife and his advisors who were doing the talking and they reminded him, that because of who Mordecai was, - a Jew - he could not win against him and that it would be the ruin of him. Zeresh, his wife, who, along with the others, had suggested Haman build a gallows for Mordecai was now telling him that *he* was doomed. Had they offered the same advice previously, Haman may have thought twice about the edict he had drawn up in the king's name. They had lived and worked among the Jews all their lives and probably had heard many stories about how God had delivered His people in the past from all sorts of trials and persecutions. It seems they had a good knowledge of God's dealings with His chosen people so why not mention this before! It's too late now, and as Haman listens to their prophecy, his mind in turmoil, his pride broken and bruised and his reputation in shatters, the king's eunuchs arrive to escort him to the banquet Esther had prepared.

What a sight Haman must have been as he made his way back to the royal palace, head bowed in shame and humiliation and probably dragging his feet. I wonder if anyone knelt before him along the way, or whether he even noticed. Once more he would pass Mordecai sitting at the king's gate, dressed in sackcloth and ashes.

Mordecai the Jew.
The despised one.
The hated one.
The one whom the king honoured.
The one who has been the thorn in Haman's side.
The one who was quietly waiting for God to act on behalf of His chosen ones.

As he walked towards the queen's private quarters, the downfall of Haman had already begun…

"It is mine to avenge; I will repay,"
says the Lord.
Romans 12:19

Heavenly Father, we stand in awe of You,
as we see Your hand of sovereignty
controlling events in the life of Haman.
We tremble at Your power,
we rejoice in Your justice,
we are humbled in Your presence,
we realise what it is to 'fear the Lord.'
Fear - not in a frightening way,
but a 'fear of the Lord'
which moves us to
honour,
obey,
praise
and glorify You
as the only wise, immortal, invisible God.

For a man's ways are in full view of the LORD, and he examines all his paths. The evil deeds of a wicked man ensnare him; the cords of his sin hold him fast. He will die for lack of discipline, led astray by his own folly.
     Proverbs 5:21-23

You prepare a table before me in the presence of my enemies.
     Psalm 23:5

Haman the Guilty One!

Esther 7:6
Esther said, "The adversary and enemy is this vile Haman."

Little did Haman realise as he walked into the palace for Esther's banquet that he had only a short time to live. He had left his home and family and they would not see him alive again. Mordecai had also seen him for the last time as he passed by the king's gate. Only God knew the outcome of Haman's wicked schemes.

Esther, undoubtedly, had prayed again as she prepared for this second meeting with the king. She had promised to make her request to him at the dinner party and she needed courage, especially when she would mention her nationality. She had no idea how he would react, but she was depending upon God and His help when she would seek the king's favour.

The moment came when the king asked Esther to make her request and, once again, he gave her the promise of, *'up to half the kingdom.'* Without hesitation, she immediately told the king the whole story of how both she and her people had been sold for destruction and slaughter and annihilation. As Esther spoke and Haman heard her reveal her national identity, he must have been overcome with shock and fear. He thought the day couldn't possibly get any worse and now this!

Esther had been very wise in asking Haman to join her and the king for the banquet, as she knew his plot would be exposed. Anything she would have to say now would be said in the presence of the king and it gave Haman no opportunity to get out of it, or even deny it.

He had nowhere to hide. Esther continued her appeal to the king by saying that if the Jews had been sold into slavery she wouldn't have bothered coming to him at all. She knew the king would be aware of the fact that as slaves, they would still be contributing to the Persian empire by their service. On the other hand, their total annihilation would mean a collapse in the economy! The Jews were free citizens and, as such, their contribution was invaluable because of their trades and occupations. Some of them also held positions of immense importance throughout the kingdom.

The three of them had just spent some time over the meal, where small talk and light hearted conversation would have taken place. They had feasted well and were now having wine. The king had been in a good mood and was looking forward to hearing what it was that Esther wanted. Haman, most likely, would have been willing the time to pass until he could go back home and regroup! Esther, with quiet confidence, had waited for the king's question. All in all, the whole scene would have been serene and tranquil.

Until now, when suddenly, it all changed!

The king's reaction was one of fury, *"Who is he? Where is the man who has dared to do such a thing?"*

Esther gave him the answer, *"The adversary and enemy is this vile Haman." (7:5-6)*

Haman's guilt was written all over his face and he was terrified before the king and queen. The king was in such a state of anger that he left his wine and went out into the palace garden ...

> **Your hand will lay hold on your enemies;**
> **your right hand will seize your foes.**
> **Psalm 21:8**

*Heavenly Father, we thank you that when we pray
and ask for courage, wisdom and victory, You deliver.
When we don't know where to turn or how to sort
out difficult situations, You take over.
When the enemy seems ferocious and threatening,
You are all-powerful.
We thank-you
that You are near,
that You care,
and that You will never leave us or forsake us.*

...judgment without mercy will be shown to anyone who has not been merciful...
　　　James 2:13

Haman Hanged

Esther 7:9
...'A gallows seventy-five feet high stands by Haman's house...'

King Xerxes realized he had been tricked by Haman and was extremely annoyed and upset. He had regarded him as a trusted friend and advisor, and had given him a position of authority. The king began to wonder if Haman had anything to do with the assassination plot which Mordecai exposed. His thoughts were going back over the times Haman had approached him to seek his signature for various purposes, especially the day when he wanted to get rid of the 'certain' people in the kingdom. Now realizing who these people were, the king knew he had been very foolish when he gave Haman his ring to seal the edict. As Xerxes paced up and down pondering all of this, Haman was inside begging Queen Esther for mercy. As soon as the king had left the room it occurred to him that Esther was now the *only one* who could save his life. He knew, full well, the king would have him executed. He threw himself down before her couch, begging for mercy. The man who had proudly and mercilessly written the death warrant for a whole nation of people was now on his knees before the *only Jew* in the whole kingdom, who was in a position to help him. Esther, who held no position of significance whatsoever in the palace of King Xerxes, had, on this occasion, Haman's future in her hands. She did not know what the king had decided to do but she did know, that should she offer mercy to Haman, he would eventually continue to carry out his evil manoeuvrings.

Just then, the king returned to the banquet hall and saw Haman falling on the queen's couch. His anger flared and he accused Haman of intending to molest the queen. As soon as he spoke, his attendants covered Haman's face! His fate had been decided.

Harbona, one of the king's attendants, told Xerxes about the gallows Haman had built to have Mordecai hanged. The king wasted no time in ordering Haman's execution as he said, *"Hang him on it!" "So they hanged Haman on the gallows he had prepared for Mordecai. Then the king's fury subsided."* (7:9-10)

Esther, the orphan cousin of Mordecai the Jew, was indeed in the palace, *'for such a time as this.'* Her courage to go before the king knowing she could be executed, was displayed in her own words, *"and if I perish, I perish."* These two people, who had continued to live in the country of their captivity, had played a vital role in overthrowing Haman's evil edict.

We praise You Lord, for Your sovereign power and control over the affairs of man.
Out of the darkness, You call forth light.
Out of evil, You bring good.
Out of despair, You bring delight.
Out of suffering, You bring glory.
In the face of defeat, You give victory.

*And we know that in all things God works for
the good of those who love him,
who have been called according to his purpose.
Romans 8:28*

Wait for the LORD and keep his way. He will exalt you to inherit the land; when the wicked are cut off, you will see it. I have seen the wicked and ruthless man flourishing like a green tree in its native soil, but he is soon passed away and was no more; though I looked for him, he could not be found.
Psalm 37:34-36

Rags to Riches

Esther 8:1
That same day King Xerxes gave Queen Esther the estate of Haman...

The law in Persia gave the state the right of entitlement to the property of anyone who had been sentenced to death for treason or any other threat to the throne. King Xerxes could keep for himself Haman's property, instead, he gave it to Esther. All that Haman had accumulated through deceit, greed and injustice, now belonged to her. If the king gave her up to half the kingdom as he had promised, Esther had now become a very rich woman. She appointed Mordecai as manager over Haman's estate. Mordecai the Jew, despised and hated by Haman, is now in complete control over everything Haman had accumulated and owned. Zeresh, the widow of Haman who had been instrumental in suggesting her husband build a gallows for Mordecai's hanging, inherited nothing. Even in this, God delivered justice.

Esther told the king, that Mordecai was her uncle and he was invited into the king's presence. King Xerxes had reclaimed the signet ring from Haman and he now took it off his finger and presented it to Mordecai. Once again, the ring was handed over, this time though, to a man who would do good and not evil. He was also given new clothing, which represented his office and his authority, *'royal garments of blue and white, a large crown of gold and a purple robe of fine linen.'* (v.15)

Mordecai, who once sat at the king's gate, was now the second most important man in the kingdom of Persia!

No longer wearing borrowed clothes, as was the case when he was led round the city on the horse.
No longer wearing sackcloth and ashes which gave definition to his deep grief.

As he stood alongside his orphaned cousin Esther in the presence of the king, both dressed in royal robes, I'm sure their hearts were warmed by the goodness and blessing of their faithful God. Whatever their spiritual state was at the beginning of this story, Esther and Mordecai had been compelled to turn to their God because of affliction. Their dependence upon Him for mercy and grace had been richly rewarded.

What a rags to riches story!

Gracious Father, we stand amazed once again at Your hand of providence.
You lift the needy off the ash heap and seat them among kings.
We praise Your Name.
Our hearts sing with joy when the enemy is defeated.
Give faith today, to any
who seem to be in an impossible situation.
Help them to cast their cares upon You.
Deliver them we pray.
May they rejoice in victory.

And without faith it is impossible to please God, because anyone who comes to Him must believe that he exists and that He rewards those who earnestly seek Him.
Hebrews 11:6

Humility and the fear of the LORD bring wealth and honour and life.
　　　Proverbs 22:4

Esther's Supplication

Esther 8:3
...falling at his feet and weeping.

Haman was dead but the edict he had delivered was very much alive! The law was such that it could not be revoked, even by the king himself! Knowing this, Esther came to the king, pleading on behalf of her people. She fell at his feet weeping, as she begged him to put an end to the edict Haman had devised. The king extended the gold sceptre to her and she stood before him. He was pleased with her and was willing to approve anything she suggested. Esther asked that he write an order overruling Haman's destructive plan. She even gave Haman his full title, *"Haman son of Hammedatha, the Agagite."*

Esther was not sitting back enjoying the benefits of her sudden elevation to wealth and power. The evil Haman had perpetrated an evil act which could still be carried out. Her family, friends and nation had been condemned to death but, she was in a position whereby she could intercede before the king on their behalf. After the king heard what she had to say, he gave Esther and Mordecai permission to write another decree, in their own words. Mordecai could seal it with the king's signet ring and it would therefore be law throughout the kingdom. They wasted no time carrying out this suggestion. The royal secretaries were summoned and Mordecai dictated the terms of the new edict. The orders were written in the script of each province and in the language of each people throughout the kingdom. *'They were also written to the Jews in their own script and language.'* (8:9)

Mordecai wrote in the name of the king and sealed the dispatches with the king's signet ring. They were then given to couriers, who, spurred on by the king's command, set out on fast horses and rode throughout the kingdom to deliver them.

Mordecai left the king's presence that day wearing his royal clothes and the city of Susa held a joyous celebration. God had turned their weeping into laughter, their sorrow into joy, their despair into hope. Their prayers had been answered far beyond their imagination, and the people rejoiced in what God was doing.

Haman's pride in himself and his own thirst for power, had been his downfall, while Esther's humility brought honour to a whole nation and praise to God.

Thank You Jesus for humbling Yourself, even to death on a cross so that we might go free.
Thank You Jesus for being our intercessor before the Father.
Thank You Holy Spirit that You intercede on our behalf, when we do not know what to pray and that Your intercession is always in accordance with God's will.
Thank You Father, for the privilege that is ours, in interceding on behalf of others.

*Therefore let everyone who is godly pray to you
while you may be found.*
Psalm 32:6

Shouts of joy and victory resound in the tents of the righteous: The LORD's right hand has done mighty things! The LORD's right hand is lifted high; the LORD's right hand has done mighty things!
I will not die but live, and will proclaim what the LORD has done.
This is the day the LORD has made; let us rejoice and be glad in it.
     Psalm 118:15-16,17,24

Mordecai's Edict

Esther 8:16
For the Jews it was a time of happiness and joy, gladness and honour.

Just over two months had passed since Haman's evil decree had been sent to all one hundred and twenty-seven provinces in the kingdom of Persia. Now, from India to Ethiopia, Jews in all the provinces began to read the new decree. Written in the king's name, by Mordecai their fellow Jew, they read, *in their own native tongue,* words which encouraged them greatly and gave them much reason to celebrate.

'The king's edict granted the Jews, in every city, the right to assemble and protect themselves; to destroy, kill and annihilate any armed force of any nationality or province that might attack them and their women and children; and to plunder the property of their enemies.' (v.11) The very words which Haman had decreed, had now been reversed, as the new decree gave the Jews of the kingdom, permission to defend themselves, on the thirteenth day of the twelfth month, the month of Adar.

Their situation would not be completely resolved for another ten months, but that did not deter them from rejoicing in their new found hope of deliverance.

The cloud of dread had been lifted. The death sentence had been removed. Instead of grief and ongoing sadness, they once again experienced great happiness and joy. They feasted and celebrated at the glad news. Throughout the kingdom there was music and singing, not only, because of the new edict, but also, because Mordecai had been raised to a position which left him highest in the land, next to the king. Only a few days before they were treated as a despised people by the evil Haman and were threatened with complete annihilation, but now, they were a highly honoured nation.

What a turn of events it was! The palace of King Xerxes was not only home to a Jewish queen, but also, a Jewish prime minister! From within its sumptuous surroundings, God had been working on behalf of His people. A holocaust had been declared but God had over-ruled and in His foreknowledge had already begun to turn it into the very place from which their redemption would come!

Gracious Father, there is no-one like You and no-one besides You.
As our Sovereign God, we give You praise.
As our Deliverer, we will shout with songs of victory.
As our Refuge, we will hide in You.
As our Defender, You cause us to stand fast in the face of the enemy.
As our Light, we walk in the brightness of Your love.
As our Strength, You lift us up when we are bowed down.
When we call, You answer.

*The LORD redeems his servants;
no-one will be condemned
who takes refuge in him.
Psalm 34:22*

The ransomed of the LORD will return. They will enter Zion with singing; everlasting joy will crown their heads. Gladness and joy will overtake them, and sorrow and sighing will flee away.
   Isaiah 51:11

The 'certain' People Increase!

Esther 8:17
And many people of other nationalities became Jews...

The dramatic turn of events came about when God's people prayed, and God in His Sovereignty, answered. Esther had asked Mordecai and all the Jews of Susa to fast, pray and plead with God, for His favour to fall upon her, as she would go, uninvited, into the king's presence. Their prayers were for God to move upon the king's heart, and that he would be compassionate towards her and extend the gold sceptre. They knew Esther had been risking her life by going and that she would lose her life if she didn't. God had answered their prayers and now they were rejoicing in the abundant blessing which was far beyond what they expected could ever happen. God had not abandoned them.

> The 'certain' people were now an honoured people!
> The sackcloth was no longer needed!
> They did not need to cover their heads in ashes!
> They did not need to walk the streets mourning over a death sentence!
> Their children were now dancing with joy instead of clinging to their parents in fear!
> Mothers and fathers were lifting their children high in the air and swinging them round and round with joyous abandon!
> Two and a half months of tears, anxiety and grief had been washed away in the flood of God's Redeeming Grace!

Their relief and hope was so evident, that all the other nationalities recognized what a loving, powerful, wonder-working God the 'certain' people served and worshipped!

What a challenge this should be to our hearts to-day! It compels me to ask, even of myself, the following questions;

Is the joy of the Lord so evident in my life?
Are others seeing the power of God revealed in me?
Do I publicly proclaim His wonders and mighty deeds?
Is my witness for my Saviour, drawing others to Him?

Let us be men and women who are not ashamed of our great, wonderful, powerful, redeeming God. May we not let world events shape our thinking to such an extent that we despair like those who have no hope. Rather, may we portray and speak of the hope we have, not only in this world, but also for the next.

As we read of persecuted Christians world-wide, may we pray for them, and remember them before God, asking for strength and deliverance in their situations.
God is able!
Even in our own homes, jobs and educational facilities where we can be criticised, ostracised and rejected for our faith, may we display the joy of the LORD and continue to share the Good News of Jesus Christ, who alone is the Saviour of the world.
We too, have much to rejoice about, and celebrate, even though our enemy is still a threat!

Rejoice in the Lord always,
I will say it again:
Rejoice!
Philippians 4:4

*Lord, we come to-day confessing
that our witness can sometimes lack joy and fervour.
The cares of this world can cause us to despair,
rather than display the hope we have in You.
Give us the grace necessary
to live the abundant life,
as citizens of Your Kingdom.
May we rejoice in Jesus our Saviour
Who has lifted us up and out,
of our miry pit of sin, hopelessness and misery.
Give us a fresh glimpse of what we have in You.
Enable us to throw off the grave clothes
and celebrate in newness of life.
Help us to pray -*
Believing!

Finally, be strong in the Lord and in his mighty power. Put on the full armour of God so that you can take your stand against the devil's schemes. For our struggle is not against flesh and blood, but against the rulers, against the authorities, against the powers of this dark world and against the spiritual forces of evil in the heavenly realms. Therefore put on the full armour of God, so that when the day of evil comes, you may be able to stand your ground, and after you have done everything, to stand. Stand firm then, with the belt of truth buckled round your waist, with the breastplate of righteousness in place, and with your feet fitted with the readiness that comes from the gospel of peace. In addition to all this, take up the shield of faith, with which you can extinguish all the flaming arrows of the evil one. Take the helmet of salvation and the sword of the Spirit, which is the word of God. And pray in the Spirit on all occasions with all kinds of prayers and requests. With this in mind, be alert and always keep on praying for all the saints.

Ephesians 6:10-18

Deliverance!

Esther 9:1
...the Jews got the upper hand over those who hated them.

The thirteenth day of the twelfth month arrived. The edict of Haman was still effective, and those who supported Haman in his hatred of the Jews gathered to carry out what the edict had purposed. On the same day, Mordecai's edict allowed the Jews to defend themselves from their enemies. For the past nine months the Jews had been preparing both physically and spiritually. They were armed and ready. Their enemies, no doubt, had expected to be victorious but now, the tables were turned. The Jews stood in the strength and power of the LORD and a supernatural 'fear' fell upon the nations around them. Already there were many throughout the kingdom who were now sympathetic towards the Jews. Having seen and heard all that had happened, even the nobles, satraps, governors and king's administrators helped the Jews defend themselves because of their fear of Mordecai, whose position, reputation and authority were being used by God to carry out His Divine will.

Nevertheless, there were many who sought to follow through on Haman's orders. In the citadel of Susa, five hundred men died at the hands of the Jews, including the ten sons of Haman. Isn't it amazing to read, that, even in the capital, there were at least five hundred who sought to exterminate Jews which included Esther, the king's wife, and Mordecai, who was now a relative of the king by marriage! No doubt, these enemies were spurred on by Haman's sons, who seemingly had the same spirit of hate towards their Jewish neighbours as had their father before them. Seventy-five thousand were also killed by the Jews in the provinces. It is obvious from these numbers that Haman wasn't the only one who hated Jews! It is also obvious, that the 'fear of the LORD' had not derailed the evil intentions of almost seventy-six thousand people! Like Haman, they were not only enemies of the Jews, they were enemies of God, having, aligned themselves with the 'Amalekite.' The Jews carried out on that day, what King Saul had refused to do all those years ago when he was told to destroy the Amelekites, but sadly, he disobeyed God's command. (1Samuel 15)

The king heard about the numbers who were killed in the capital and having told Esther, he then asked her if there was anything else she wished to petition him for. Knowing that there could be sympathisers of Haman's cause still in the city, she asked that the king give permission for the Jews in Susa to have one more day to defend themselves and have this included in the edict. He gave his permission and commanded that this be done, and on the next day, three hundred died while attacking the Jews!

Throughout the provinces, the Jews were already feasting and celebrating the victory God had given them over their enemies, while in Susa, their fellow countrymen were still being attacked. In the citadel of Susa, it had been necessary to assemble on two days to face the enemy, and then, on the fifteenth day they too, rested, and made it a day of feasting and joy. In all of this, not one Jew died! Amen and Amen.

Thank you Father that we, Your children,
are highly favoured,
greatly blessed
and deeply loved.!

Ah, Sovereign LORD, *You have made the heavens
and the earth by your great power
and outstretched arm.
Nothing is too hard for you.
You show love to thousands but bring
punishment for the fathers' sins into
the laps of their children after them.
O great and powerful God, whose name is the*
LORD *Almighty, great are your purposes and
mighty are your deeds.
Your eyes are open to all the ways of men;
you reward everyone according to his conduct
and as his deeds deserve.*

I am the LORD,
*the God of all mankind.
Is anything too hard for me?
Jeremiah 32:17-19,27*

But let all who take refuge in you be glad; let them ever sing for joy. Spread your protection over them, that those who love your name may rejoice in you. For surely, O Lord, you bless the righteous; you surround them with your favour as with a shield.
     Psalm 5:11,12

The Feast of Purim

Esther 9:26
Therefore these days were called Purim.

Twelve months previously, the wicked, evil, Haman had issued an edict which intended to bring about the death of every Jew throughout the kingdom of Persia. The estimated number of Jews in Persia at that time was approximately, two to three million. His edict not only ordered their deaths, but also, to plunder their goods. This would have made Haman a very rich man. At that time, he had promised the king that he would put ten thousand talents of silver into the royal treasury for permission to destroy the 'certain' people in the kingdom. The plundering of their goods would have provided amply for this. Now, the Jews had an opportunity to increase their wealth when they put to death nearly seventy-six thousand people who stood against them, *'but they did not lay their hands on the plunder.'* (Ch.8:10) Perhaps they were reminded of King Saul, who had lost his crown for taking the plunder. Saul's disobedience did not allow for any kind of celebration, but, on this occasion, celebration was the order of the day!

A day which had been intended for doom, death and destruction, had been turned into a day of joyous celebration. God wants His people to boast in Him and not in ourselves and Mordecai and Esther did exactly that! They wrote letters to all the Jews throughout the provinces of King Xerxes, to proclaim a two-day holiday every year on the fourteenth and fifteenth days of the month of Adar. The two days would be days of remembrance, feasting and joy. They were to give presents of food to one another and give gifts to the poor. These days were to be called, Purim, taken from the Babylonian word *pur* which means, *lot*. It began with Haman when he cast the *lot* to determine the day when the Jews would be destroyed. Little did he realize that his planned day of holocaust would end up being an annual holiday for the Jews! Mordecai had all of this recorded in the chronicles of Persia, and Esther endorsed it. Although the feast of Purim is not one of God's appointed feasts as laid down in the Book of Leviticus, it is an annual celebration which has continued right up until this present day.

It begins with a day of fasting on the thirteenth of the month in remembrance of the date when Haman issued his evil decree. In synagogues all over the world, on the feast of Purim, the fourteenth and fifteenth days of the month of Adar, the book of Esther, along with the account of Moses and the Amelekites, is read aloud. Every time Haman's name is mentioned, the children stamp their feet, hiss and boo, while the adults shout out, *"May his name perish!"* They enjoy two days of feasting, giving of gifts and sending to the poor and needy gifts and food also. The whole holiday gives God the glory for His great deliverance from destruction. It reminds their children year after year of God's faithfulness, love, mercy and grace.

> ***The L*ORD *has done great things for us,***
> ***and we are filled with joy.***
> ***Psalm 126:3***

*Father we thank You for those times we can come
aside and remember Your goodness to us.
Thank you for that day in our lives when You opened
our eyes to Your great salvation.
Thank You for the many blessings You give us day by
day; homes, jobs, friends, family...
Thank You for Your grace, love, mercy
and faithfulness.
Thank You for the invitation to Your table where we
remember the death of our Saviour and Lord on our
behalf.
Thank You that one day,
He is coming again!*

Therefore, as we have opportunity, let us do good to all people, especially to those who belong to the family of believers.
      Galatians 6:10

Mordecai's Success

Esther 10:3
...he worked for the good of the people and spoke up for the welfare of all the Jews.

Mordecai the Jew is the real hero of the story. He stood against the wickedness of proud, self-indulgent, power-seeking Haman, even though it threatened a whole nation with death.

He had faith enough to believe that God would vindicate his decision.
He realised that Esther's position as queen, was for a purpose.
He made sure that Esther understood the role she needed to play.

All in all, Mordecai was a man who knew his place in the overall plan of God and he played his part willingly and sacrificially. Now, he was seated at the right hand of the King of Persia! God had richly rewarded him. Rather than use his position of authority in the oppressive way Haman did, Mordecai helped his fellow countrymen and worked for their good. The story of Esther ends with Mordecai and his dealings towards his own people. He represented them in court and spoke up for them in disputes. He made sure they were treated fairly and with dignity. His job would have included raising the funds necessary to run the country and it is quite possible he suggested to the king, the new taxation system, in order for him to bring in the reserves needed. As they were no longer under the threat of death, the Jews could continue to work, earn money and prosper, and their prosperity would have added to the prosperity of the kingdom in general.

Esther, the daughter of Abihail and orphaned cousin of Mordecai, who had been obedient to his instructions when she first entered the palace by not revealing her nationality, continued to listen and obey her cousin. Out of respect for Mordecai, her faith in God, and the *power of love* she had for her people, she had risked her life to oppose the wicked, evil, Haman, who was completely motivated by the *love of power.*

The book of Esther began with King Xerxes celebrating himself! He bragged for one hundred and eighty days, of his wealth and all he had acquired; of his kingdom and the splendour and glory of his majesty. His anger new no bounds and his lack of integrity wasn't lost on those who used him for their own ends. The king, in his anger, had removed Vashti his Queen and subsequently had her replaced.

What he failed to reckon upon was, that there was One greater than he, whose splendour, majesty, power and might were unparalleled. It was God, in His Sovereignty, who had placed Hadassah (Esther) into the palace of King Xerxes, *'for such a time as this.'* He who knows all things, had already known of Haman's vile and wicked schemes and God was ready for that day when the palace of King Xerxes of Persia would become,

Esther and Mordecai's House of Redemption

*"Who am I, O LORD God,
and what is my family,
that you have brought me this far?"*
1 Chronicles 17:16

*Praise be to you, O L*ORD*,*
God of our father Israel,
from everlasting to everlasting.
*Yours, O L*ORD*, is the greatness*
and the power
and the glory
and the majesty
and the splendour,
for everything is yours.
*Yours, O L*ORD*, is the kingdom*
You are exalted as head over all.
Wealth and honour come from you;
you are ruler of all things.
In your hands are strength and power
to exalt and give strength to all.
Now, our God, we give you thanks,
and praise your glorious name.
1 Chronicles 29:10-13

*You intended to harm me,
but God intended it for good
to accomplish what is now being done,
the saving of many lives.
Genesis 50:20*

I trust you enjoyed the visit to

ESTHER & MORDECAI'S

House of Redemption

Marion